Praise for *Higher*

"I purposely took forever to finish this book because I didn't want it to end. A book that gave me peace of mind. A book beautiful inside and out. I highly recommend *Higher* by Charles Hanna to anyone who wants to find greater beauty, meaning, and success in their life. Happy people like the way things are and they look forward to change. Unhappy people don't like the way things are and they do not like change."—TUMBLR

"A great starting point for anyone who wants to make significant change in their life. Hanna guides us past the thoughts that hold us back from becoming our best, happiest, and most-fulfilled selves."—ROSE CAIOLA, FOUNDER OF REWIRE ME

"Candid, eye-opening, and insightful."—MNI ALIVE

"This is a book that is worth a second read and one that I will be keeping on my shelf after I loan it to some family members to read. If you are feeling stuck in your life and you are not sure what the problem is or what to do next, *Higher* may be just what you need."—SMS NONFICTION BOOK REVIEWS

"Wonderful for those in early recovery, and long-term recovery, and anywhere in between."—SERENE SCENE MAGAZINE

"Whatever you're going through, whatever you're experiencing, I would really recommend this book."—DR. JEANETTE GALLAGHER, WELLNESS RADIO

"I would recommend this book to anyone in recovery, no matter what stage or step they are at. I would also recommend this book to anyone searching for a deeper meaning in their life. Hanna provides readers with practical and practicable techniques and ideas so that everyone can apply the Higher way to their daily routines and to their dreams. An uplifting and inspiring book... Five stars, a definite must-read."—FRASER VALLEY NEWS

"If you find it hard to believe that a life of luxury will not magically make you feel happy, Hanna does a good job of explaining why this is the case. I believe this is an incredibly important thing for most North Americans to understand."—HEALTHY LIFE LESSONS

"For some people, it takes hitting an all-time low to discover real happiness. Charles Hanna shares his personal experience with life management, as well as his climb toward true freedom after his life had taken a dark turn to addiction and self-doubt. Hanna explains how finding our Higher Purpose actually allows us to use our personal demons to become our best selves."—CONSCIOUS COMMUNITY MAGAZINE

"I found it particularly helpful that he shares the tools and attitudes that have helped him sustain recovery and to have a more fulfilling life. It was deeply inspiring to read about his honestly accounted struggles and how he turned his life around, learning to be mindful and to surrender to a higher power to find peace in all situations (note: this is not a 'religious' book at all, and he mentions that you can apply the principles no matter what your religion or spiritual orientation). I have already started implementing what I've learned from this book as an experiment in my own life."—GOODREADS

"The book is, in a great way, highly provocative... It made me challenge my perceptions. And it provides real answers... e.g., the Inner Child Meditation and powerful analogies. The author shares his life—challenges and all. I was left relating to his human-ness yet feeling awed by such a level of consciousness, and an incredible intelligence/creative ability to convey his story. Highly recommended."—AMAZON REVIEW

"The first time I read *Higher* I was on a long car trip, so I read it out loud to my husband as we drove. We paused often to discuss points the author covered. We had fantastic openhearted conversations that gave us new ways of looking at our lives. I've now read the book a second time, underlining and making many notes in the margins. I haven't experienced addiction and recovery, but I deeply resonated with so many things in this book, and I was left feeling hopeful and more connected than I've been in a long time. If someone like Hanna could face such unbearable losses in every aspect of his life and come out of it with a new perspective and passion for life, then what's my excuse?"—AMAZON REVIEW

"*Higher* is packed full of useful information and should probably be read a few times to really grasp, or even in bits and pieces. I will read it again for sure."—B. MCAFEE, TV PRODUCER

"I think people who are focused on growth, development, and balance would find the book to be a good read. People who can admit that we aren't born knowing how to stay focused, avoid pitfalls, believe, and follow a clear path, will be drawn to this book."
—J. EGO, ENTREPRENEUR

"I found myself aligned with much that the author shared with the reader: his thoughts on life, business principles, and how he ultimately found himself as he put more trust in a greater power."
—F. LITWIN, ENTREPRENEUR

"I think *Higher* is outstanding and could help many, many people. I especially liked that the author told personal stories of his journey and his own perception disorder so that readers could identify with him and feel that their own struggles have hope, given that Hanna was about as low as one could get and still found a new way."—H. GOUDGE, FAMILY LAW COUNSELOR

"I found the voice in which it was written to be refreshing, vulnerable, and very intimate and, because of that, quite powerful. Anyone who has struggled with their own lack of success will likely be inspired by the prescriptions the author offers to achieve happiness, peace of mind... and a higher perspective. The big takeaway I had upon reading *Higher* was that life is so very precious and that being in awe of every breath is a path to the deepest divine gifts. And there is hope for anyone struggling to arrive at this perspective."—S. HANNA, ENTREPRENEUR

"I found this book inspiring because I was able to make sense of some of the things that have hindered me. For example, losing momentum because of distraction. I enjoyed the discussion on the gift of life especially. I have battled depression in the past and had lost sight of this gift."—M. YOUSSEF, STUDENT

"I really loved the Inner Child Meditation technique and the notion of a personal support group. Practical techniques like those are valuable takeaways for the reader in a book like this."
—L. POWER, INVESTMENT EXECUTIVE

"I have enjoyed every second of the book and find it full of interesting information that parallels what I have been slowly learning over the years."—K. MORRISON, INTERIOR DESIGNER

"I believe that *Higher* may help a lot of people to navigate their way through the most troubling and darkest times, or alternatively avoid making mistakes that could be painful."—T. JIVOV, REALTOR

"I always feel when a book makes me stop reading and reflect on what was said and how the thought resonates with me a deep and potentially growing moment. I found quite a few of those moments reading this book."—T. WARBURTON, ENTREPRENEUR

"I found that during and after reading it, I was and am consciously more grateful for all the things that are right and good or perfect in my life and less bothered by the very few things that are negative."—W. MCCARTHY, IT EXECUTIVE

"I'm sending this book to one of my sons, who struggles with perception about himself and the world around him, in hopes he will gain something from it."—M. FRASER, PSYCHOTHERAPIST

"This book is helping me before I go to bed. I don't feel so afraid and alone."—S. CONTE, ITALY

"Inspiring and insightful read, which I'm sure I will use in my own search for a higher existence. Thanks for your honesty."
—M.K. SMITH

"I think the author is courageous to have shared so much of the profound pain and joy life gave him, and the lessons learned along the way. It will definitely make people reflect on their own lives and help them gain new perspectives."—L. BOYD, MUSICIAN

"What an amazing story. He was meant to live. He was meant to live to tell this story and to do this book."—KMET 1490 AM, LOS ANGELES

"I am getting all sorts of texts as we are talking about this guy and his book *Higher*. It does not get more real than this."
—CHAD BENSON, CHAD BENSON SHOW, NEWSTALK 1290

"The book was very enlightening for me. It reinforced what I do right and caused me to think about where I am lacking."
—T. HEINTZBERGER, ENGINEER

"I am really enjoying this book. The writing style is vivid and eloquent. I can picture the scenarios and empathize with how the author must have felt. This doesn't happen very often."
—A. VANOVA, ART GALLERY OWNER

"*Higher* is an insightful and inspirational tool for anyone looking to improve their way of life and live more consciously. Charles Hanna, through his own life experiences and great suffering, has deciphered ancient spiritual teachings and translated them in a very accessible and meaningful way. He teaches us the true concept of oneness, of a higher power, and that we are all truly connected. It is our misperceptions and identification with our experiences that cause us to suffer and feel separate from that greater source."—C. SAVOIA

"I truly think this is a must-read and I intend on suggesting to my friends that they purchase it."—E. RICHMOND, BUSINESS OWNER

"I've given extra copies to people I felt would benefit from reading *Higher*. I have implemented the Inner Child Meditation—so powerful. It has enabled me to overcome obstacles I didn't even know I had."—L. HELGESEN, BUSINESS MANAGEMENT

CHARLES HANNA

Higher

AWAKEN TO A MORE FULFILLING LIFE

Figure.1
Vancouver/Berkeley

17 18 19 20 21 5 4 3 2 1

Cataloguing data available from Library and Archives Canada
ISBN 978-1-77327-039-5 (2nd Edition pbk.)

Editing by Alice Peck
Copy editing by Lesley Cameron
Proofreading and indexing by Stephen Ullstrom
Design by Jessica Sullivan
Front cover images: table and akileb / photocase.com
Author photograph by Warren McCarthy

Printed in the U.S.A.

Figure 1 Publishing Inc.
Vancouver BC Canada
www.figure1publishing.com

I dedicate this book to
my daughter Darcy, without
whom I might not have made it
through my darkest time.

AUTHOR'S NOTE

I have tried to recreate events, locales, and conversations from my memories of them. In order to respect and maintain anonymity, in some instances I have changed the names of individuals and places and other identifying details.

Contents

2

Finding Our Higher Perspective

3

Finding Our Higher Power

4 Finding Our Higher Purpose

5 A New Way of Life

6 Living Twenty-Four Hours at a Time

7 Spirituality versus Progress

8 Closing Thoughts

Foreword

/

I MET CHARLES HANNA in 2005. He is a special man in many ways—blessed with intelligence, possessed of keen awareness, and capable of tremendous insight about people as well as the world. Life is about experiences, but unless we are particularly aware, most of us take them for granted. This is not true for Charles; he remains determined to see the gift in every experience. He has taken the time to document many of his most important realizations in this glorious compilation of essays that encourages us to look at our lives and appreciate them in new ways. Perceptive and prescriptive, *Higher* is a guide to a better, more connected, and vibrant way of being.

Writing a book that would be of benefit to others has been one of Charles' long-term goals and *Higher* is the result. Giving back is critically important to him. So is empowering people to reach a higher level, hence the name of the book. I believe that Charles has achieved his goals in a manner with which readers can connect.

Higher is a book that challenges each of us at a very basic level—and it will challenge you. Each page will urge you to question your values and encourage you to examine your relationships, your spirituality, and your purpose. Best of all, *Higher* will help you live a fulfilling life and become the person you were intended to be.

DAVID FEDER
counselor and therapist

Introduction

/

April 17, 2017

WRITING HIGHER HAS been more gratifying than I could have imagined. I experienced tremendous personal growth as a result of reflecting and incorporating the book's important life lessons into my daily life. I also reread it periodically because it helps me apply its principles to what's new in my life.

Moreover, my friends and family now hold me to a higher standard. One that is very challenging at times. For example, if I get upset in any way or don't respond promptly to a friend's message, then I am quickly reminded of what I say in the book about Higher Perspective and love. In turn, I laugh and remind them of the other pages where I talk about the importance of self-care.

Most gratifying, however, was the feedback that I received from many readers. Some told me that it was life changing and that their friends noticed those changes. One example is a distant relative in her mid-sixties who was always very quiet and withdrawn, perhaps because of a strict upbringing. She wrote to say that she'd read my book and that it had helped her, and she thanked me. A couple of months later, I met her at an event and she looked radiant, hardly the person I had known. We talked, and when I asked her why she liked the book she answered, "It gave me permission to love myself." That really hit deep.

Another surprise was the number of couples that read the book together, sharing stories. It seemed to renew an enthusiasm about life they once shared a distant time ago. What these particular experiences helped me realize is that when relationships break down, more often than not it is because the individuals have broken down. As they lost their joy for life, so did they lose their joy of love and connection. This made me realize that to rebuild a broken relationship, a couple need to build themselves individually first. Chances are they will rediscover that spark that once drew them together in the first place.

The most notable change that I personally experienced is how I started to see all challenges as messages and opportunities to develop something that I had never even thought about. I am stunned by how often what I may have previously perceived as "bad" turned out to be a blessing in the end. My daughter Darcy expressed her surprise at the way I handled the loss of my iPhone during a recent visit to LA when I reacted by saying, "Maybe it is a good thing," and then worked to make it so.

With respect to my future plans, my focus is on making available to as many readers as possible the tools I describe in *Higher* so that more people can benefit from them. Surprisingly, many people do not have the patience or time to read; hence, I am working on an audio version of the book for release in 2017. Also, to create awareness I am sending a free copy of *Higher* to all major counseling and education institutions in North America.

There are many other activities in the works, including new Higher Retreats, seminars, my presentation at ideacity 2017, and my website, www.higherbook.com, which features podcasts, videos, and news. You may also find me on social media, including Facebook, Twitter, and LinkedIn.

However, what I am most excited about is a new shorter handbook based on the principles of *Higher* for adolescents in middle and high school. This is the most fragile and impressionable age, when one influential statement at the right time might change a life. Our children are dealing with greater challenges than ever before, because of increased population, technology, and social media pressures. They need grounding and the ability to take over their own care as they quickly transition into adulthood. I hope to publish this new booklet in late 2017.

Please reach out to me via email—Charles@higherbook.com—with any feedback or questions that come up for you as you read *Higher*.

Thank you, and enjoy your journey to a Higher Perspective.

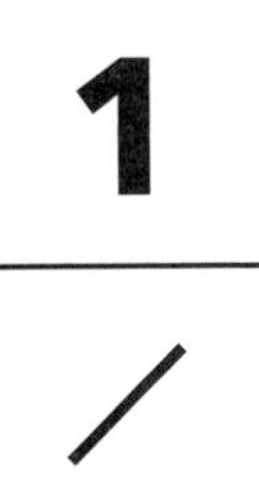

The Journey to Higher

Life is an incredible gift filled with joy and fulfillment. If you do not experience this on a sustained basis, then *Higher* is the book for you.

SO OFTEN, WE FOCUS ON THE MUNDANE or on day-to-day tasks. We think of our worries and of the possessions we believe will make us happy. We dwell on our resentments and on the people and things that frustrate or anger us. We are often consumed by pettiness and completely miss what a magnificent day lies before us. This is normal human nature for many of us, and we all need guidance to learn to remember and appreciate our gifts.

The world's great philosophers and spiritual leaders all teach us that happiness depends on how we look at life. I am certain we can change our outlook. By finding our Higher Perspective, Power, and Purpose, we can challenge our beliefs about life and the pursuit of happiness.

In this book, using examples I've gleaned from my experiences of despair, addiction, and accomplishment, I'll show how the Higher Perspective can help you go beyond a life of shortsightedness, judgment, and a self-centered viewpoint wherein you see yourself as the center of the universe, evaluating everything in terms of its being good or bad for you. Much has been written about this topic—a Higher Perspective is far easier to discuss than to accomplish. I'll explore why only a small fraction of people are capable of a sustained wider perspective and how you can become one of them through simple changes to your daily routine that will help you expand your attitudes and position you naturally in this sustained state.

A connection to and an understanding of a Higher Power has been the goal of humankind from the beginning of time. Ever since humans developed the ability to think cognitively and abstractly, they have searched tirelessly for their origin and purpose and the one supreme creator at the source of it all. Through myths and religious beliefs, most people have developed either faith in a God or confusion about or outright rejection of the idea. In this book, I'll examine the concept of a Higher Power apart from any religious orientation. I'll provide a framework upon which you can build your own sense of self and purpose, live in the moment, and enjoy the wonder of life as it is and as it is meant to be.

Higher goes on to explore ways in which we can identify and pursue our Higher Purpose in light of our changed perception and understanding of the meaning of life. Once we truly see ourselves within the wider perspective of the universe, our role and function within it becomes clear. Spiritual growth contributes to happiness and when combined with fulfilling our Higher Purpose, it provides the ultimate gratification.

Most motivational talks and books inspire only for as long as we're hearing or reading them, and then we return to our old ways of thinking and being. This is because there is a difference between having a realization or awakening and living in a state of spiritual consciousness. In the last section of *Higher,* I present a template with tools for how to sustain a state of joy and growth. These tools include practical changes to our attitudes, goals, and behavior that can result in a revolutionary shift in our levels of serenity, sense of inclusion, and happiness.

As you read, you may start to appreciate that you do not "own" yourself, and that you were created with specific attributes, in a specific place, at a specific time, and for a specific reason. You are "free" to do as you please, but you have a cardinal responsibility to protect and nurture yourself. I hope that *Higher* will guide you in that. ■

Keep an Open Mind

If you are genuinely seeking a happier life or simply a different way of looking at the one you have, keep an open mind as you navigate this book.

WE ARE ALL likely to judge and dismiss concepts that are foreign to our way of thinking. With pre-established and ingrained beliefs about core topics such as God and addiction, we tend to disqualify much of this information because we feel it does not relate to us, or because we do not expect to learn anything new. However, while reading these pages, try to see past the way you have always looked at things. The concepts discussed herein require openness to a new way of thinking. If you find yourself disagreeing with, disqualifying, or simply not relating to a particular point, just make a mental note of it, put it aside, and continue to read with an open mind. You will find that by doing so you may relate strongly to something surprising and perhaps will subsequently examine your core beliefs in a different light.

In particular, I discuss the concept of God throughout the book, but it is important to note that it is not in relation to any religion. The word "God" conjures up a variety of preconceived notions, but I mean it as the Higher Order to which we all belong. Regardless of religious orientation—whether we believe in a Supreme Being and intelligent design, a spiritual concept of a Higher Power, or completely random processes—most of us know that we are part of something much bigger than ourselves. I use the word "God" to refer to that bigger perspective, whatever it may be for you. Therefore, as you read, you may replace the word "God" in your mind with Higher Power, Higher Order, Good Orderly Direction, Love, Life, or whatever term you prefer.

It is also important to remember that we are all much more alike than we might think, regardless of our demographics, be they religion, race, or social position. Even identical twins can have completely different circumstances and values depending on how they are raised. Our differences pale in comparison to the common threads that we all share as human beings. Our struggles, just like our diseases, do not discriminate, and it would be a huge tragedy if our disinclination to relate to each other robbed us of the vast wealth of life lessons that we can share. So, as you read, try to relate to the emotions and responses, even if completely different circumstances trigger them for you—they may become relevant later, or may guide you as you help someone else who is suffering. ■

Addiction Is Perception Disorder

Just as space exploration helped develop technologies that could be applied to everyday life on Earth, our exploration of addiction and recovery helps us understand the origins of serenity and happiness for everyone, even those not afflicted with the disease of addiction.

CONTRARY TO WHAT most people think, the direct experience of many recovering addicts shows that addiction is a disease of perception. In fact, it would be more accurate to refer to it as a perception disorder disease. In its advanced active phase, it may manifest itself in extreme substance abuse, which is the association most people make. However, its causes are established during childhood and the effects are always with us.

There is evidence to suggest a hereditary predisposition to substance addiction, whereby the body fails to completely metabolize drugs such as alcohol, causing an irreversible byproduct accumulation in the brain. Over time, when an invisible threshold is reached, the use of drugs becomes unpredictable and uncontrollable because of this accumulation. Once this happens, lifetime abstinence becomes a prerequisite to any recovery. In other words, abstinence is not recovery; it is only a prerequisite to recovery.

The underlying perception disorder was present before the abuse and simply became exacerbated by it. This disease can also manifest itself through behavioral disorders such as compulsive gambling, working, sex, love, eating, and codependency, for example. Most people do not realize the broader spectrum of addiction and how prolific this perception disorder is—abuse is not necessarily uncontrollable, and many people can abuse without actually being addicted. We do not have to abuse substances or engage in compulsive behavior to suffer from various degrees of perception disorder.

Perception disorder is a condition whereby we view ourselves as the center of the universe. Everything is seen largely from our personal perspective and evaluated in terms of being good or bad for me. For example, we may enter a room and hear people laughing, and assume or fear they are laughing at us. Our partner may need to talk to a friend, and instead of considering their need, we automatically conclude that they do not trust us or value our opinion or that they just want to get away from us. We may speak to a group on an important issue but lose focus, becoming more concerned with the impression we're making than the subject matter. These skewed perceptions result in skewed emotions and responses that, over time, could materially deteriorate our quality of life.

Perception distortion results in what might look like abnormal behavior and feelings, when in fact it could be perfectly normal, depending upon the situation. For example, suppose someone is swinging a bat and shouting in anger, and you erroneously perceive they are coming after you; or perhaps the attack is real, but the threat is blown out of proportion by you. You may react with fear, possibly even attacking the person. Another individual, watching and seeing that no hostility was intended and that your reaction was unwarranted, might speak out against you. Already angered by the perceived attack, you will now feel more confused and hurt by the unfair criticism.

Without dialogue or the open exchange of thoughts and emotions, these resulting negative experiences are not corrected. In cases that lead to addiction and substance dependence, the perception distortion is severe and progressive. Over time, and through repetition of such confusing experiences, an individual becomes increasingly isolated from society until the pain is so great that substance use and/or compulsive behavior becomes a distraction, a welcome relief, and ultimately a necessity.

If one were writing a questionnaire to detect the presence of this disorder, it would include questions like, "Do you think of yourself or have others described you as self-centered, too sensitive, too negative, too afraid, childish, or said that you worry too much, lack empathy, are close-minded, or feel shame?" Regardless of your circumstances, if your natural predisposition is to feel ungrateful or unhappy, then you probably suffer from perception disorder to some degree.

Perception disorder develops during childhood within dysfunctional families. I'd define a dysfunctional family as one in which a child is robbed of their childhood and left feeling marginalized and unloved. Or the child may be loved, but, for whatever reason, is not given adequate attention and time for intimate talks throughout childhood to help them integrate into society with proper grounding. Such a child is unable to share their feelings openly, and this sets the stage for the development of distorted perceptions of themselves and the world.

In extreme cases, these children become acutely insecure and vulnerable as they grow into young adults. The first time such children experience the numbing effects of any sort of drug or potentially addictive behavior during adolescence they may experience incredible relief and a sense of belonging that invariably initiate their dependence. Only a small percentage become severely addicted, but no one has perfect perception and even a minor distortion compromises our ability to lead the best life possible. We don't have to be an out-of-control substance abuser to benefit from a correction to our perception disorder.

Through my own struggles with addiction and recovery, I had to learn to understand and navigate acute perception disorder. This helped me realize how self-centered perception affects all of us. Whereas it means life and death for an addict, for everyone else it can mean the difference between happiness and mere existence, or the difference between sadness and outright depression. Perception disorder is hardwired and forever influences the way we perceive our lives, but we can make corrections to greatly offset its negative effects. This is why it is important to understand our selves and develop the tools for a Higher Perspective in our daily lives. ■

My Path

I've chosen to share the story of my failures and successes–all of which contributed to my understanding of Higher Perspective, Power, and Purpose.

WHEN I WAS fifteen years old, my family emigrated from Egypt. I was fortunate to grow up in Canada, where I completed my undergraduate studies in physiology and pharmacology, and my postgraduate studies in cardiology and neurophysiology—at which point I realized my true passion and path, and switched to marketing, business, and computer science. Having been blessed with strong interpersonal and technical skills, I was able to construct and communicate visions in simple and powerful ways, and by the age of twenty-nine, I had established my own business, was responsible for dozens of employees, and had made my first million dollars.

I was fortunate to achieve success early in life, and this helped me realize that accomplishments could not bring the happiness I sought. I struggled with this realization, and nearly died from a serious cocaine addiction. A lot of damage happened during my seeking, but miraculously I survived—and grew spiritually and professionally through my recovery.

Sometimes the worst thing that can happen is for our lives to be just "good enough," because then we aren't motivated to search for more. To see the beauty of our existence we must be forced to step back, be objective, and look at life from a distance. My total defeat led to serious searching, which caused a fundamental shift in my perspective and a spiritual awakening far bigger than I ever expected to find.

In this process, I discovered that the harder I worked to distinguish myself, the more isolated I became. I discovered that I am just a human being and therefore equal to all humanity. This led to a great sense of belonging and empowerment. I recognized there was an infinite wisdom in life—one that even the most brilliant and enlightened human being could not teach. I had a choice to either live life fully or waste it futilely. We would be far wiser to focus on and learn how to enjoy the gifts that we were born with than to squander our days in pursuit of possessions. I believe that despite what may have gone wrong in our lives, what damage to ourselves or others resulted, and what opportunities we have missed, anyone can lead a beautiful life starting right now. We just have to decide to do it.

Sharing what I have learned has always been my goal. In this book, I strive to integrate spirituality with science and common sense, just as I integrated interpersonal considerations with technical considerations in my business. I am at peace with my weaknesses, my defeats, and my blessings. I have tried to present them all openly and without reservation. The rest is up to you. ■

Beginnings

For me, there was only one direction: forward.

I WAS BORN in Alexandria, Egypt, into an upper-middle-class Christian family in the 1950s. Soon after my birth, my seven-year-old sister died from polio, which devastated my parents. My dad, who loved my sister more than his own life, was forced to keep himself together for the sake of the family; my mother was on suicide watch. While my mother was grieving, my nanny became my primary caretaker and I cried if anyone else tried to hold me.

In the years that followed, our family began to heal. My mother became pregnant again and gave birth to my sister Denise. Another year passed, and my youngest sister, Mimi, was born. I developed a strong bond with Mimi, who became my best friend and soul mate. This was probably the happiest time of my childhood, but when I was seven years old and Mimi was only three and a half, she suddenly developed a fever on a Friday and died the following Monday. It was believed to be meningitis, but it was an incomprehensible death nonetheless.

You can imagine what that did to our household. To this day, I grieve for Mimi. And not only did I lose my sister and closest friend, but I also lost both my parents once again. They were inconsolable and despondent, and my mother's anguish cast its shadow over our family for many years. I dove deeper into my own private world. By the time I was ten years old I had already developed such extreme ambition, determination, and independence that I no longer felt connected to anything or anyone around me. I just wanted to get away and be on my own when I grew up.

During middle school, I spent all my allowance on comic books that contained beautiful images of life in the West. I admired the toys, cars, people, and homes nestled among trees peacefully blanketed by snow. It was everything that Egypt was not—it was the mid-1960s, political and religious turmoil was brewing, Jews and Christians alike were being persecuted, and the threat of war with Israel was imminent. I started to live for the day that we might move away.

Just before I turned sixteen, I got my wish. My family emigrated to Montreal in Canada.

It was a true culture shock. Although we had led a comfortable life in Egypt, Egyptian law at that time meant we were not allowed to bring many of our possessions with us. Moreover, my father could not find employment for over a year. This was a hard time for us—a time of scarcity, cold weather, and cultural isolation. In addition, we not only had to learn a new language, we also now had to do household chores—in Egypt we had been lucky enough to have help in that regard, so it was quite an adjustment. Still, I had no desire to go back. For me, there was only one direction: forward.

When I was seventeen, my father moved our family to Toronto, where he finally found work. My parents wanted me to respect Egyptian traditions, while I yearned to get as far away as I could. They often proclaimed that their sacrifice in leaving Egypt was to provide "the children" with a better future, so when I did not conform, I was made to feel responsible for their losses. I became estranged from both my parents and my culture, and I resolved never to be seen as "less than" or to need anyone ever again.

As a student at the University of Toronto, I immersed myself in my studies. I was articulate and attractive and I became popular with my peers, especially the girls. I began dating, and every relationship provided a new experience that allowed me to explore my own developing sense of self. I had no intention of settling down, but at the start of my second year of college, I met a girl named Peggy. She was dynamic and beautiful, and as fate would have it, our relationship was a pivotal one in my life.

Peggy and a couple of her friends introduced me to marijuana. I had never touched any alcohol, let alone drugs, until then, nor had I ever imagined doing so. I will never forget the first time I got high. It was magical! I'd been living in a black-and-white world until then and now everything was in color. I had been listening to an AM transistor radio my whole life and now everything was in stereo. My ideas and dreams, my friends and girlfriend were all amazing—nothing short of breathtaking. I was Dorothy newly landed in Oz. I could not wait to explore every inch of this marvelous new way of being.

With the controlled use of marijuana, I was able to study for prolonged periods. I looked forward to spending all night at the library, immersed in biology, biochemistry, genetics, and more. My marks reflected this immersion and I received a major scholarship to continue my studies. By the time I graduated, I was devoted to two things: my future success and Peggy.

I continued my postgraduate studies in cardiology and neurophysiology and considered a career in research or medicine. However, I chose neither. I thought that research would fall short of satisfying my personal needs, such as more interaction with people and significant monetary success. I was also unsettled by the prospect of becoming a doctor because, while the cause was gallant and could be extremely gratifying, it was nonetheless engulfed in an inordinate amount of pathology and suffering. Since the gift of life comes with the gift of freedom of choice, I decided to seek another path.

Instead of healing sickness, I yearned to inspire healthy people to lead better lives. I made a paramount shift in my career and left medicine and the sciences to pursue an MBA in marketing and finance. At the age of twenty-four, I joined IBM, the most successful marketing organization of its time. I spent my first year at IBM training in Atlanta, Georgia, where I studied business automation and sales techniques. While I excelled technically, my greatest interest and passion was sales.

After two and a half years, it was time for me to move on. By the time I was twenty-eight I had started my own business. I was finally free to implement my ideas, and I found and addressed a huge unsatisfied demand in the IT market. I took pride in providing a valuable service with the highest degree of professionalism and integrity.

Peggy was a part of my life throughout this time. I believed that she shared my dreams and was devoted to me, but I was still unsure about committing to one person. I thought a change of scene would help me decide if what we had was real, so I went on a vacation to Martinique with a buddy. During that trip, I got more than I bargained for—I was introduced to cocaine.

My experimentation with cocaine started innocently, and as ridiculous as it sounds, I never believed it would be harmful.

I was unaware of what addiction was—not only had I never seen it in any of my relatives or friends, but this was the 1970s and drug use was not yet rampant or regularly in the news. In fact, I'd read in a 1967 edition of a pharmacology reference book that cocaine was a safe drug that temporarily enhanced the IQ. As with marijuana, I believed cocaine to be a valuable tool that could help me develop my vision for my life.

However, I couldn't control my cocaine use as I had with my marijuana use, and my dependence escalated. The drug made me feel like Superman. In my euphoria I decided that Peggy was the love of my life, and despite my fear of loss and abandonment rooted in the deaths of my sisters, I believed her devotion would keep me safe. There was neither reason nor room for insecurity, conflict, or mistrust. I was ready to commit. In October 1981, at twenty-nine years of age, I married Peggy.

I was empowered and in control of my destiny. I was completely happy and in love with my wife. My business was expanding rapidly. I was inspired by and inspiring to my employees, and by the age of thirty, I was making millions and was on my way to exceeding all of my boyhood dreams. I felt invincible, yet paradoxically it was the beginning of the end for me.

Peggy and I didn't turn out to be the team I thought we were. Moreover, my family responsibilities had increased. I was now financially responsible for my parents in their retirement years, and I employed not only my sister, but also other members of my extended family. My career success had trapped me in a life that was completely opposite to the life of freedom and independence I had envisioned.

Shortly after I turned thirty, Peggy became pregnant. This caught us completely by surprise, but we embraced the news and even cut back on our use of recreational drugs. When our daughter Darcy was born, Peggy and I fell completely in love with her, but apart from loving my daughter and taking pride in my continued business success, I continued to become everything that I never wanted to be.

The wakeup call came one evening when my daughter was eighteen months old. As I went to bed, I reflected on how fortunate she was to be healthy and beautiful, born to two loving parents who could afford to give her the best life possible. However, as soon as my head touched the pillow, I sat back up and said aloud, "Oh my God! Her father is a cocaine addict." ■

Living, the Dream

Even though I didn't always know it, I have been living my dream since the moment I was born, through good times and bad, and will continue to do so until the day I die.

I'VE HAD MANY dreams, and I have always considered myself one of the most ambitious people I know. I was on a constant quest for honest success and improvement that could better both society and me. I dreamed of helping others through my passions and succeeding materially as well. Like many people, I considered financial success important because it yields significant power, influence, and freedom.

It wasn't always like this. In terms of accomplishing "my dream," I had not only succeeded in the most difficult part of the journey, I had also gained the absolute confidence that I would accomplish everything else I set out to do. The result? I ended up in a deep depression. But why?

After my initial joy on the way to achieving my first great milestones in family and business, and soon after getting there, I felt great excitement and hope. My passion fueled my drive and euphoria. However, it didn't take long before I realized that everything felt the same as before. I was restless and wanted more—nothing had changed. Success did not translate into the bliss I had somehow imagined it would. If anything, I had added the worry of mismanaging, and possibly losing, all I had accumulated—my business and my family. This was why I fell into a depression. Until I achieved material success, I thought I had a good compass and knew where I was going, and that gave me drive, hope, and a sense of adventure. However, once that compass proved to be faulty, I was lost, without any idea of how to achieve happiness or reach that state of bliss that I had dreamed about and thought was the meaning of life.

How can someone who seemingly has it all end up on a self-destructive path? People always wonder how anyone who is blessed with success and fame could be unhappy or ungrateful. Think about the tragic deaths of people like Robin Williams, Whitney Houston, Amy Winehouse, Heath Ledger, and Philip Seymour Hoffman. The question most people ask is: How can they blow it after achieving such success? The answer—for me, anyway, and the point I make throughout this book—is that nothing compares with the gifts of life that we are all born with, and if something happens in our development to rob us of the ability to enjoy them, then no amount of wealth or fame or looks can make up for that. My story begins with abandonment by my grief-stricken mother, and when my resultant extreme fear was triggered at the height of my success, I crumbled.

Another thing to note is that during the active phase of addiction, the mind of an addict works to sabotage its own recovery. Again, people always wonder why anyone who is destroying themselves does not stop, or at least seek help. The answer has to do with how the mind looks to everything but the obvious, and why addiction is often described as the only disease that convinces you that you do not have it. In my case, my perception of reality kept me fighting, even as it became slowly obvious that I was doomed, in much the same way that frogs do not jump out of water that is being gradually heated to a boil.

Finally, I want to share the intimate details of my struggles because after years of reflection and hard work I now truly know myself, I am not afraid of being open, and I want to help others as best I can. It is fear of the unknown that prevents most of us from risking exposure to scrutiny. Most people have never been examined publicly and called out on their most vulnerable and shaming acts the way addicts are in treatment. As you'll see, my program of recovery demanded nothing short of total transparency and scrutiny from counselors and other recovering addicts, as I took full responsibility for past events and future healing. This realization and acceptance of one's shortcomings is painful and humbling, especially for addicts who tend to be particularly self-centered, egotistical, and sensitive. I am comfortable revealing everything because I became intimately familiar with who I am and what I learned from all of my experiences—the good and the bad.

Today, I am blessed with love and respect for and from my family, my friends, my community, and—most of all—myself. I live with the comfort of knowing that all I have to do is the next right thing, and everything will be the best it can be and as it should be. ■

What Is This Dream?

The dream is the acceptance of the extraordinary gifts bestowed upon every one of us, at the right time and at the right place and with all the right components. How lucky can anyone be?

THE DREAM IS that I am alive! I hit the mother lode of all interstellar lotteries. Against all odds, and with infinitesimal probability, I was born at a time when things could not have been any better for human beings. Not only am I healthy, which is worth more than all the money in the world, I also live during a time when humans are the dominant species, with 7 billion of them working tirelessly to make life as beautiful and convenient as can be.

I would not sell my eyes for all the money in the world—and neither would I sell my health or mobility; my children, family, or friends; or my freedom or purpose in life—none of it, ever! Imagine having inconceivable riches in return for total isolation from humanity—never seeing, touching, or communicating with any other human being for the rest of your life. I cannot imagine wanting to make such a trade. Human contact alone is worth more than all the money there is.

Think of the love of children; the unconditional affection of pets; the warmth of the sun and the splendor of the sky, oceans, and beaches; or the beauty of music and great works of art. Think of the advances in science and medicine that can improve the quality of life—but remember that they can't guarantee a world without overpopulation and the resulting impact on the environment.

In almost every other time in history, life was too hard, and in the future it might be as well. We have been given an oasis where we have the opportunity to flourish—at the right time, in the right place, and with all the right things. How lucky can anyone be? Now *that* is a dream come true. We live it every day—but how many of us realize it? ■

My Descent

My intention in writing this book is to pass on my life lessons, not my life story, but I believe that hearing how my journey took me to the extremes of despair and success and ultimately toward spiritual understanding may help others to find their own Higher Perspective, Power, and Purpose.

WHEN I WAS in the midst of it, I thought my drug abuse was due to stress caused by my lifestyle and circumstances. My business and personal relationships began to spiral out of control—although I was oblivious. When one of my most trusted employees suggested that I go to a treatment center I was astonished. It certainly never occurred to me that I might have a problem. Nonetheless, I was willing to do anything to end my misery, and so, at age thirty-three, in September 1985, I checked myself into a three-week inpatient program at Bellwood Treatment Center in Toronto. I found it to be the most depressing hospital imaginable. There were classrooms, counselors, and other patients, and I was bewildered by having to be in that environment and increasingly frightened and angered by what I learned about myself.

Bellwood introduced me to Alcoholics Anonymous (AA). AA is a fellowship of people with a common desire to stop drinking or using drugs by adhering to a twelve-step program of recovery (the Twelve Steps). When I realized the potential harm my behavior could inflict on my daughter I stopped using everything; by the time I left rehab I considered myself "cured."

In June 1986, Peggy and I had a big party. I was married to a beautiful woman and my business was thriving. It had been nine months since I had touched cocaine, but a friend brought some to the party and I ended up doing a few lines. It was a great night, but I vowed never to touch the drug again. That is, until my friend called me a week later at the office, and I picked up the phone to say "No," but the word "Yes" came out of my mouth instead. Within weeks my slip led to smoking coke, and I knew I was in deep trouble. I contacted Bellwood to readmit myself, but they had no spots available for months. This was the beginning of a steep decline.

The following years were the worst of my life. My dabbling in drugs for fun turned to substance abuse, which increased in direct proportion to the growing turmoil in my marriage. I spent most of this time under the influence of drugs and I was lucky to survive. Several trips to different treatment centers had no lasting effect and I fell deeper and deeper into cocaine addiction. It systematically destroyed every aspect of my life, and many of the people I trusted most took advantage of my sickness to betray and cheat me.

When my marriage finally disintegrated, I realized I had run out of excuses and vowed to quit cocaine on my own. And I did... until five weeks later when my mother died. Her sudden death had a profound effect on me because she died while watching my life fall apart. Yet, my sorrow unearthed an anger about my childhood that I had not realized I harbored against her, leading to a relapse and a coke binge so extreme that I was unable to attend her burial.

Feeling completely disoriented and unable to express my anguish, I sank deeper into depression and addiction. I remember telling a friend that I felt like I was buried alive in a coffin six feet underground and no one could hear my screams from the grave. I was fading away.

A few more trips to rehab didn't help. When I reached the point of envisioning suicide, I went to see an addiction expert who recommended a four-month treatment program. I told him it would be hard for me not to see my daughter for that long and I was not sure that my company could survive my prolonged absence. The counselor asked me how old I was. I said, "Thirty-six." He then asked me how old would I be when I finished treatment, and I replied, "Thirty-six." He said that was not long at all to save my life after this multi-year downward spiral. I agreed to go, but not right away—I still had personal business to settle and a company to run.

Shortly thereafter I was home alone. I looked in the mirror and told myself that if I could only stop my cocaine use now I could persevere. I wanted to escape my yearning for Peggy. I was smoking cocaine at this point, and in a fit of desperation or perhaps vengeance I took a huge toke in the hope of breaking loose from my sorrow. The effect was the opposite of healing—I collapsed onto the floor. A powerful spasm made my hands clench and then slowly started to travel up my arms. I lay frozen in horror as the spasm kept going, past my elbows and then my shoulders and then into my head. I went completely deaf except for a faint high-pitched noise in my ears. My breathing grew shallow and my pulse became a hardly perceptible vibration.

I was about to die. I was consumed with fear as I prayed, "Please, God, don't let me die this way. I don't want my daughter to grow up without her daddy and hearing that he died a junkie." I lay there, paralyzed, in total silence for what seemed like an eternity. About twenty minutes later, the spasms began to reverse until I was able to stand up, and then, in a trancelike state, I reached for my pipe and another toke.

For the following two months, I tried to hang in as best I could while I prepared my company for my departure to the treatment center. My depression was tremendous and I had never felt so isolated. I could not believe how my whole world—family, friends, and employees—had turned against me despite my trying to be kind, having the best of intentions, and contributing so much to so many. This left me shattered. What had become of my belief that I had to stay independent? ■

The Turning Point

Nothing short of complete surrender could make my spiritual awakening possible and give me the ability to accept a fundamental shift in perspective–from self-centeredness to an external grounding.

I WILL NEVER forget the day—January 5, 1989—I waited to board a plane to the treatment center. I started getting high on New Year's Eve and did not stop. When I left for the airport, I had not slept or eaten for five days. I am six feet tall and I weighed 127 pounds! I looked and felt like a concentration camp survivor. The skin on my shoulder blades was as thin as cigarette paper. I was frightened, disoriented, and rabid with anger. I was leaving nothing behind; I had lost everything, including myself. I was bankrupt physically, emotionally, and spiritually. I was without hope, but somehow I kept going.

On the airplane, I began to cry uncontrollably. A flight attendant asked me what was wrong, and all I could say was, "I lost my daughter." She left me alone with my grief.

At the rehab center, after a day of detox, my assigned counselor met with me and asked me to tell her my story. My eyes filled with tears. I was overwhelmed with pain and didn't know how or where to start. I told the counselor that I had been to five other treatment centers and they had not worked because no one could answer my question: Why had the people closest to me betrayed me? I guess what I wanted was someone to understand my anguish and validate my misery.

The counselor listened carefully. At my first pause she leaned toward me and said in a solemn voice, "I see tombstones in your eyes." Just like that, she discarded me and everything I had said, and then stood up and walked away.

I had been in a place of complete defeat and hopelessness. I hadn't imagined it could get worse. The counselor was my last lifeline and it had just snapped. I could hear no sound and feel no breeze. I had no tears left. All I could do was try to take my next breath. I cannot remember the next twenty-four hours.

I am only alive today because of the miracle I experienced on my third day in treatment. As I entered my room and walked by the mirror, I glimpsed something I had never seen before. I jumped back to take a second look but it was gone. Gone but not forgotten. It was like the movie *The Fly*, where the man is lost within the monster. For a split second, I saw that monster. In that moment I realized that I was possessed by a demon: addiction.

I spent the whole night writing and crying, and described myself as a burning ship that I had to abandon. The following day, I realized the only hope I had for saving myself from my disease was to not use my mind at all! I could not think for myself. I could not question anything that my counselors told me to do. I could not even trust my own eyes or ears. The best way that I can describe it is that this disease consumed me entirely and used all my intelligence, experience, resources, determination, and willpower against me. It shaped my perception of reality to isolate and destroy me. The tools that I had always relied on and that had helped me succeed and distinguish myself—my intelligence, charisma, loyalty, and determination—became weapons that my addiction used against me, leaving me with no hope of fighting it on my own. My mind was the enemy.

I surrendered completely and abandoned my old self without any bargaining, or even remorse. In fact, I experienced hope for the first time. I was awakened to the fact that my salvation was only possible if I allowed others—my counselors—to guide me back to life. What I experienced and the things I discovered on my journey are the heart of this book. ■

Surrender

When that deafening shriek of addiction is finally silenced, life presents us with the miracle of a new beginning. Life proves once again that it is forever beautiful, no matter where we go. Like a child, completely trusting and open to learning everything, we are born afresh.

ADDICTION IS A progressive disease of the mind. In its advanced stages, there is absolutely no hope of recovery or happiness without complete surrender and reliance on outside guidance, yet the Achilles heel of addicts is the relentless determination to think their own way out of situations. However, if the mind is diseased and their best thinking got them into trouble in the first place, how can they help themselves?

I was like most people—my mind had always been my most reliable asset for maintaining control. I was successful in business because I was ambitious and capable and determined never to give up no matter how challenging things got, so the notion of surrender went completely against my grain and everything that I wholeheartedly believed in. Surrender meant defeat and was for losers.

Toward the end of my addiction, I believed that my mind was the only thing that I could trust. Maintaining control was like having my feet planted firmly on the ground; it was my sense of gravity. Imagine if gravity were switched off and you began to float away without any power over where you were going or what you might hit. I cannot imagine anyone willingly letting go in that way. Even at the lowest points of my addiction, as I came close to facing total destruction, I found myself holding on for dear life. However, complete surrender meant that even hanging on would not suffice. This darkest moment and (hopefully) bottoming-out for an addict is a point of absolute and utter fear. It was not until I had nothing and nobody left to lose that I could have my epiphany of being "possessed" by the demon of my disease, which allowed me to finally and completely let go of my addiction.

It is hard enough to walk away from all your material and sentimental possessions, but it is a whole other level of difficulty altogether to walk away from all your emotional and intellectual possessions. Imagine letting go of everything you ever believed in and ever loved and your entire conviction and familiarity with life. My mother, my sisters, my soul mate, my daughter, my self, and all my love and memories and ambitions and hopes—my sense of everyone and everything that I ever knew and believed in and lived for were gone!

True surrender eludes most addicts, as it had eluded me. Nothing short of a complete surrender could have made it possible for me to have my spiritual awakening and accept a fundamental change in my perspective, frame of reference, way of thinking, and priorities. That's how I moved away from my belief that I was the center of the universe to becoming open to and then achieving an external grounding and frame of reference. I stopped thinking for myself. I did everything that my counselors at the treatment center told me to do without question. Surrender was the essential foundation of how I saw everything else that came after my epiphany. I saw everything in a new light. Things that were not obvious or were seemingly immaterial before took on a completely different meaning for me.

I was completely humbled, scared, and lost. I could not see what lay ahead. I was told about a Higher Power in my AA meetings and group sessions but I did not understand it, let alone feel it or believe in it. The counselors told me, "Fake it until you make it." I did, because, frankly, I had no other choice at that point. Then, somehow and perhaps miraculously, I started to see it. I started to feel *my* Higher Power and I came to believe. In other words, it was not because I intellectualized a better way ahead that I let go; it was only because I had no choice but to flee the burning building I had locked myself in. It was only after I let go completely that I began my journey and could ask, "What now?"

The rest of this book is aimed at exploring the lessons that I learned from my Higher Perspective on life. ■

Beware the Addict

Addiction is cunning, baffling, and powerful, and even after my surrender it kept trying to manipulate my mind to make me slip and destroy my recovery.

SHORTLY AFTER I went into treatment for the final time, so did my wife, Peggy. Darcy went to live with her maternal grandparents. A few weeks later, I became convinced that Peggy's father must have abused her and now my child was helpless in that same household. I started to go nuts and wanted to leave the center to save her. She was all that mattered—an innocent, helpless child whose only hope was for me to save her from this horrific prospect. I was just about to prepare for my departure when it hit me: my disease was using my tremendous love for my daughter to trick me out of treatment.

It did not even matter if my fear was well founded (and today I have no real reason to believe it was)—the disease will use and distort reality. However, when a population is quarantined for an infectious disease, you cannot risk letting anyone out even if you are confident an individual is not infected. In the same manner, my true surrender saved my life that day when I did not trust my mind to leave. My only option was to get better and trust that God would take care of her. Had I left, she would not have had a father at all.

If you have a substance abuse problem, then above all tackle that first. No matter what else is going on, nothing will help you and those you love more than arresting the disease. ■

A Spiritual Awakening

I came to understand that I was just a human being and nothing was greater than that. What followed was a tremendous sense of belonging and empowerment.

THREE MONTHS AFTER rehab, I was at an AA meeting listening to a speaker. I cannot remember the exact words, but as he described hitting bottom, the gravity of my situation struck me. I realized that no matter what I did and no matter how I tried to follow to the letter the teachings of AA and everything I learned in my recovery, I might still not be able to save myself from my deadly disease. I knew that I had no more chances left. I was lucky I had made it as far as I had and I believed that if I fell one more time I would die very quickly.

I started to cry uncontrollably. It was a large, open meeting, and it was not my turn to speak. I was seated somewhere in the middle of the auditorium and started to weep from my core out of fear such as I had never felt before. I wept out of sorrow for myself, for my life, and for my little daughter. Everyone I had trusted had abandoned me. I was lost and overcome by horrifying fear and sorrow.

This was my moment of spiritual awakening. People who sat nearby immediately surrounded and embraced me. I cannot remember anything that was said to me but I felt unconditional comfort, love, and care as I had never felt before. Humbled by my defeat, I was completely naked—no longer hiding behind my accomplishments and pride—yet at this time of complete humility and nakedness, I was able to feel this incredible love, acceptance, and sense of belonging. I was nothing more or less than a human being. I may have been hurt and defeated, but I was a human being with no facade and that was all it took for me to be able to be loved and cared for unconditionally.

The magnitude of that moment lingered as I absorbed its meaning and ramifications. I started to see that I was just a human being and that there was nothing greater than that. I was essentially like everyone else—and that meant that I was as great as all humanity. What followed was a sense of belonging and empowerment. I was able to receive love without questioning whether I deserved or had earned it, and I started to believe that the people around me genuinely cared about me and hoped that I'd succeed in my recovery. I was one of them. It was then that I realized I was not alone, not on my own. I believed for the first time that I could stay sober if I kept completely humble, honest, and true to my recovery. What followed was a renewed enthusiasm for life and all its gifts. This spiritual awakening changed my core. I developed real love and respect for myself, and most of all, became grounded by the belief that no matter what happened I would be okay. ■

Humility and Selflessness

The more humble and selfless we are,
the more connected we become, the more we have
in common, the more we relate to one another,
and the more we can give and receive.

MANY OF US are familiar with and admire the "Peace Prayer" of St. Francis of Assisi:

> Lord, make me a channel of thy peace;
> that where there is hatred, I may bring love;
> that where there is wrong, I may bring the spirit
> of forgiveness;
> that where there is discord, I may bring harmony;
> that where there is error, I may bring truth;
> that where there is doubt, I may bring faith;
> that where there is despair, I may bring hope;
> that where there are shadows, I may bring light;
> that where there is sadness, I may bring joy.
> Lord, grant that I may seek rather to comfort than to
> be comforted;
> to understand, than to be understood;
> to love, than to be loved.
> For it is by self-forgetting that one finds.
> It is by forgiving that one is forgiven.
> It is by dying that one awakens to eternal life.

This prayer teaches us that it is better to give than to receive, better to love than to be loved. I have come to realize that the magic lies in neither giving nor receiving more than someone else, but in just being human. When we are humble and selfless, we become the essence of our selves, able to give and receive freely. The state of being totally humble and selfless without ego is our shared essence, and we become as one—both giver and receiver simultaneously.

I once heard someone share that while he believes people care about others in general he does not believe they care about him "specifically." The reality is that the more individualized we become, the smaller the number of people who can relate to us. Conversely, the more humble and selfless we are, the more we have in common with others, the more connected we become, the more we can relate to one another, and the more we can give and receive simultaneously. We can tap into the vast richness of being part of the world at large. Conversely and paradoxically, the more we distinguish ourselves even through our perceived successes, the more disconnected we become from others.

When I understood this, I could not help but think of how cruel I had been to myself before my surrender and spiritual awakening, all the while thinking I was practicing self-love. I used to tell myself that I did not deserve to be complimented because I was capable of more, and only when I was on top would I deserve praise, love, and approval. Even then, no matter what I achieved, I just raised the bar again and expected even more of myself.

I now understand that it is by nurturing and reinforcing a sense of belonging rather than by comparing and pushing that we sow the seeds for great connection, freedom, fulfillment, and surprisingly, attainment. ■

The Inner Child Meditation

Thanks to Inner Child Meditation I am not the person I once was. I have become more self-sufficient, because it taught me to develop an intimacy with myself, freeing me from the need for outside affirmation or recognition.

MY REALIZATION THAT I had to nurture myself was the start of an epic journey with my Inner Child that helped me to love myself and never feel alone. Through Inner Child Meditation, I was able to process my painful memories and thus start to heal emotionally and to feel naturally happy once again. There is a wealth of material on the Internet that can help you understand the benefits of Inner Child Meditation. For a more scientific explanation, please refer to works such as *Affect Regulation and the Repair of the Self* by Dr. Allan N. Schore of the David Geffen School of Medicine at UCLA, an internationally recognized expert in neuroscience. Here, I'd like to explain my experience with Inner Child Meditation, how it was particularly powerful in my recovery, and why I believe it is crucial if we want to develop love, respect, and compassion for our selves.

During my drug treatment, a counselor who saw that I was struggling introduced me to Inner Child Meditation. He had me sit down across from him. After getting me to calm down and take deep breaths, he coached me through a visual meditation. He had me close my eyes and imagine finding a place of solitude in my mind. I visualized that I was walking on plush, deep-green grass in a beautiful garden within a forest. I relaxed and imagined the scenery. He then had me go through some trees toward a beach where I could hear waves breaking. As I approached, I saw a small child near the water, playing in the sand. The counselor asked me to approach the child. As I drew closer, he told me that the child was me as a five-year-old.

When I saw "me," tears started to run down my cheeks. I cried because I felt such sorrow for that little boy. I had been through so much pain and this helped me remember how I had started out as an innocent little child who loved life but somehow, and despite the best of intentions, was abandoned and hurt. The counselor told me that this child had been abandoned for a long time but now he had me. I was now the parent and should embrace the child (myself) with love and assurances that he/I will never be abandoned again. I will never abandon him again. I will never abandon me again! This was the start of an epic journey with my Inner Child. It helped me to love myself, enjoy my own company, and never feel alone again.

Why did Inner Child Meditation work for me, and how can it benefit you? In my Inner Child Meditation, I effectively separated my emotions from my intellect, which allowed me to see things more objectively and with compassion. I saw part of myself as a child with a spectrum of feelings that could range from bliss, serenity, and gratitude to hurt, defeat, and hopelessness. I also saw another part of myself as the adult with an intellect separate from my Inner Child. I was able to caress myself and give myself the same sort of guidance, love, and care I would give my little daughter. For example, if I was hurt because someone had done something nasty to me, I would never advise my Inner Child to be angry or to seek revenge, or to go tell that person off and do what comes naturally when my self-centered emotions and fears are triggered!

This practice works because I am not only getting the proper advice, I am also giving it. I feel it and believe it—and this changes me. When I meditate with my Inner Child about a difficult situation, I am able to not only incorporate the Higher Perspective in the outcome, but also process my feelings and develop lasting relief and peace. I'll share some real examples of how these meditations helped me during particularly hard times in my life and recovery.

I was once severely hurt and shamed when people I trusted took advantage of my vulnerability. Often, memories of this event would be triggered and result in pain that I saw in my Inner Child when I approached him in my meditation. I found myself embracing my Inner Child and assuring him that whatever those people did was their issue and not a reflection of his self-worth, and that it should not make him feel ashamed or question who he was. I knew—and I told him—that he was a beautiful soul but had not been appreciated or understood and that was their loss. I continued by owning up to our mistakes and assured him that even when we make mistakes we can correct them, learn from them, and try to make sure we do not make them again. My good qualities will flourish even more with the wisdom won from these hard experiences. This meditative process took away the shame and feelings of hopelessness from those particular memories.

Another time, I triggered my most painful childhood memories when I thought of the worst act of betrayal and abandonment that I had ever experienced, one by some of the people closest to me. I found my Inner Child banging his head against the walls of a little room. I could see dents and blood running down his face because of his desperate attempts to stop his emotional pain. It was devastating to watch. I was at a loss as to how to even begin to articulate my feelings, let alone deal with them. I was frightened as I approached him, because for the first time I had no idea what to say to make it better or to make sense of it. As the parent, I felt helpless, afraid that I would not know where to find the strength to help my Inner Child through this. I was only able to hug him and rock him back and forth as I tried to quiet him down. I cried with him—and this is when the magic happened. I found myself remembering what I had learned about trauma and telling him that when people go through a trauma together it creates a powerful bond between them. As I wept, I continued to say aloud, "I cannot imagine any situation that could be more difficult or hurtful or senseless than what you and I are going through right now, but just think of how much closer together this will bring us." It was a powerful moment, and from the depth of my despair I found the beautiful gift of bonding with my Inner Child at a deeper level than could have been possible any other way. That bond was more important to me than the awful experience. The bad memory became the bridge that blessed me with this gift, and it never hurt me again.

Another time, I was extremely tired and could not imagine how I could do the Inner Child Meditation, but I knew I had to force myself because I had promised my Inner Child that I would check in with him every night. No matter how hard I tried, I could not meditate; I was completely spent. I was upset that I had allowed myself to become too tired to do the meditation, but most of all I was afraid that I would knowingly let my Inner Child down for the first time, and that scared me. I never wanted to fail him. So I tried again, and again, and then I just ran straight up to him and held him and said, "I'm sorry, I'm just tired. Don't you ever let anyone or anything make you think that I don't love you because I couldn't come to you tonight as promised." Here is where the powerful shift took place. As I embraced him, in my exhaustion I could not help but think of all the times when others were not there for me when I needed them. I always thought it was because they did not love me or care enough. Now I could see that they had their own limitations that may have had nothing to do with me. I also remembered in dismay the times when I was particularly hurt and angry and needed them to reach out to me repeatedly as I repeatedly rejected them, while still wanting and expecting them to continue to reach out repeatedly to help me feel assured of their love for me. I could now see how unreasonable and childish I was. From that point onward I did not feel needy or judgmental if someone was not always there for me when I needed them. Instead, I recognized the challenges in their lives that had little or nothing to do with me.

The bottom line is that the Inner Child Meditation provides an invaluable tool to process hurtful triggers of memories from the past that may cripple us. Every time I had one of these memories, it would trigger feelings of shame, anger, and hopelessness. Yet, when I meditated over each one individually, I could process them into something positive, and as I did so, the hurt associated with each one was taken away. They no longer hurt me.

I cannot remember how many triggers I had when I started. It seemed like hundreds, but I am sure there were just a few dozen key ones. Over the span of three or four months of daily meditation in the morning and at bedtime, I processed all of them and began to feel my joyful self come back to life. Within a span of a few months, I started to regain my positive outlook, confidence, and sense of humor.

Here's a story that demonstrates the magnitude of my change. A few years after I surrendered, I found out about a large competitor in my industry that was up for sale. Ten companies wanted to buy it, including a few of the giants in the IT business. My chances were next to zero, yet somehow I managed to inspire its management and they helped me structure the winning deal. It was an industry coup, and the day afterward I was sitting in my office radiating joy, pride, and euphoria from the magnitude of my achievement. I'd accomplished as much success with this one deal as I had in my previous seven or eight years of work combined. Then it hit me. I broke into goose bumps. I realized to my shock that I had not shared my story of this victory with a single soul. I never even thought about doing so with anyone as a way to prove myself. The point I want to make here is that I had always been the opposite of that; in the past I had always needed to announce every accomplishment or failure to be able to handle or savor it.

Thanks to Inner Child Meditation I am not the person I once was. I became more self-sufficient and so no longer need anyone's affirmation or recognition to feel good. I know now that this is a direct result of the intimacy I developed with myself. I am content to embrace myself and hug my Inner Child with approval. I used to think that I had to share everything for life to be meaningful, but I discovered the difference between the joy of sharing and the need for sharing. Now I share more openly than ever, not because I need to impress or to feel loved and admired, but out of a sense of belonging and to find my Higher Perspective. ■

2 / Finding Our Higher Perspective

No matter what our self-centered perception tells us, life is a treasure. We have everything we need.

WE WAKE UP MOST MORNINGS COMPLETELY oblivious to the miracle of miracles that it takes to make a new day happen. Yet, every moment has the power and potential to transform our lives completely. At the very least (and barring crises and catastrophes), there is no reason why we cannot experience utmost joy and gratification every single day.

Normally, we focus on our chores and routines instead of our fortune of having a life and a purpose and the ability to live them. We worry about and focus on what we believe we must have to be happy. We may dwell on our resentments and the people and things that frustrate us or worse, and too often we're consumed by pettiness. All of these states of mind can cause us to completely miss the magnificent day that lies before us. This is normal human nature, but with guidance we can learn to always remember and appreciate our gifts.

Our Higher Perspective is our ability to see our lives and our selves in the context of the entire universe. By so doing, we realize that almost everything that happens to us and around us is part of a larger order and has little to do with us. This helps us to live in harmony with the universe. We develop a less self-centered point of view and stop feeling responsible for everything that affects us or consumed by trying to control it. ■

The Gift of Life

Each one of us received life free upon birth. Free! No one was asked to pay for it. No one was told what to do with it. This priceless gift was given with no expectation of anything in return.

THERE IS A truism to describe someone who is in a state of bliss: *They don't have a care in the world.* No matter who we are or where we are from, I am sure we would all agree that it is a pretty good goal and that it says that in the absence of worry, life is pretty good. In other words, we do not need to acquire things or status to achieve freedom from worry. Life is as good as it can ever get all on its own if our happiness is not sabotaged by fears, angers, and resentments.

Look at what life gives us. Every morning we wake up because a trillion things happen perfectly that enable us not only to breathe and be conscious, but also to explore and interact with the world and to enjoy our senses of sight, smell, taste, hearing, and touch—any one of which is worth more than all the money we can imagine. Consider it—would you trade your eyesight for a billion dollars? How about the ability to fall in love? What is that worth?

It is not just our senses, it is also the richness of what we can freely enjoy with those senses—beautiful skies, sunsets, oceans, and all the awe-inspiring beauty of nature. Not to mention the people with whom we share our happiness and experiences, strengths, and hopes; with whom we fall in love; and with whom we share protection and support. What about the privilege of having plants for our medicines and food? Or the love and devotion of pets? Have you ever considered what an incredible gift it is to have a soul look at you for its every need and devote its entire being to loving you and giving you company—unconditionally? Then, of course, there are children and the immense blessings they bring. Think about the absolute trust placed in us by the universe—we are honored that so many of us are blessed to have a child whose growth we can shape to the best of our ability. Our gifts are many and great.

And what about the time and world we are living in? Every one of us could have been born at a different time and place with nothing compared to what we have here and now. Just consider history alone—Earth is about 5 billion years old, and so the odds of being born at this time instead of at any other time are perhaps 500 million to one! We have better odds of winning a huge lottery prize.

I suppose what amazes me the most as I consider our immediate and wider blessings is that 6 to 7 billion people are alive today and so many of them are working to make our lives better, producing art, clothing, medicine, and housing, and working in agriculture, transportation, technology, and government, to name only a few sectors.

Yes, each one of us received life free upon birth. No one was asked to pay for it. No one was told what to do with it. This priceless gift was given with the expectation of nothing being offered in return. Something made this happen and for that I am eternally grateful.

Once, several years ago, I was walking in the streets of Egypt when I came upon a blind man dressed in a dirty *galabeya* (the traditional men's clothing in Egypt) and wearing dirty pieces of cloth instead of shoes. I heard him muttering to himself, "I thank you, God. You who are kind and merciful." This brought tears to my eyes, because he had gratitude for his life even though he had no wealth, power, career, or importance—not even his eyesight.

Sadly, it is usually only after great losses that we learn to appreciate the worth of what we have. No matter how rich we might be, or smart, fast, powerful, or good-looking, and no matter how much we lose and how hard that may be, the sheer magnificence and quantity of all our basic gifts of life make all that pale by comparison. Being connected and feeling grateful for my blessings is what spirituality has come to mean for me and what my Higher Perspective helps me to experience on an ongoing basis. ■

Things Are the Way They Are Supposed to Be

Nothing is forever lost or damaged;
eventually, somehow, sometime, somewhere,
it will all appear perfect again because
it always was, always is, and always will be.

THE MORE I work on my understanding of life, the more I see that everything is the way it is supposed to be and that it could not be any better. If you looked at it from a Higher Perspective, you would see that this lifetime is only a very small part of our existence, and no matter how tragic it is, we must believe that it is part of something bigger and eventually, somehow, sometime, somewhere, it will all appear perfect again because it always was, always is, and always will be.

Let me use a tree as a metaphor. During the holidays, I often find Christmas trees frustrating because the branches are not spaced evenly to allow for optimal placement of ornaments. I used to think, "Wouldn't it be nice if all the branches were exactly three inches apart and at 120 degree angles as they spiraled evenly up the trunk?" Instead, in real life, they are randomly spaced and sized. Sometimes there are big gaps between the branches and even large spreads without any branches at all. Conversely, sometimes branches are close together and even clumped in groups. But if I were to step away from the tree and look at it as a whole, and then step even further back to look at many trees in a glade or a forest, it would become obvious that the trees are all perfect. Mother Nature is perfect and there is nothing that I could possibly do to make Her better.

And if I were able to change the spacing between the branches and make them even, what would I destroy in the process? Countless things that rely upon this natural formation would be affected. For example, birds may need clumps of branches to take cover and support their nests and habitat. Likewise, they need spaces between branches for sunshine and so that they can fly to and from their nests. So, clearly, we cannot just change the order without unknown, unexpected, and possibly dire consequences.

Even if we could make that change without disturbing the natural order of everything else, would it look better? I once visited the island of Martinique a couple of years after it had suffered a direct hit by a fierce hurricane. I saw thousands of new trees that had been planted. They were all in straight rows, equidistant from one another. As I drove by them, I could see them all line up and then move apart and then line up again perfectly from another angle. I could not help but miss the beauty of nature's random placement. The placement of these trees looked fake and man-made—not pretty or magical. Even if I could change the shape of branches and make them perfectly symmetrical per my design, they would not look or be as lovely in the end as I hoped.

Let us go one step further and imagine that we could space the branches, not affect the balance, and make them look just as pretty as nature does. How much energy would we have wasted? Instead of enjoying what nature gives us for free, we would have squandered that gift and wasted our time and energy focusing on something completely unnecessary. We could be focused on enjoying trees as they are. We could be enjoying the wonder of creation rather than being consumed with pointless and fruitless pursuits. Every tree has a unique formation that is natural and comforting, and it's senseless to erase its distinctive signature for anything else.

Let us apply this way of thinking to ourselves. Looking at the Christmas tree close up and evaluating its flaws is similar to looking at life from a self-centered perspective. We dwell on so many things that could be better or are missing altogether, comparing what we have to what others have. We may have been told many times that the grass only seems greener on the other side but that does not stop us from seeing the flaws in our own lives or immediate surroundings. The only way we can see the true beauty of our existence is by stepping back and looking at the world from afar. That is what I refer to as the Higher Perspective.

Two of my sisters died young, well before their time. I was one year old when my older sister died. I cannot remember her, but I experienced the pain of her death through my parents. When I was six years old, my younger sister Mimi died. I remember her well and still mourn her death. I have always felt intense pain and experienced a sense of injustice for their short lives. Why did they have to die so young? Why my family? Why both sisters? How can anyone reconcile an unspeakable tragedy such as a child's death?

It is impossible for me to understand the way the universe works, but I am beginning to see that it all works perfectly and exactly the way it is supposed to. Even its apparent randomness and what we might consider its many faults have meaning and purpose.

Who is to say that my sisters' short lives did not embody perfection or have not created something even more beautiful elsewhere that I cannot fathom? We transform from life to dust and from dust to life again. The cycle goes on and on in ways we cannot begin to comprehend. Every life and spirit and energy contributes to this life and to the next one.

Perhaps it is also a crucial lesson that we cannot take life for granted, no matter how much we believe we are entitled to any aspect of it, and that we need to learn to feel more gratitude for all our blessings. Huge losses will always cause unspeakable pain, but I find solace in knowing that, overall, nothing is completely lost or damaged and that eventually—somehow, sometime, somewhere—it will all appear perfect again because it always was, always is, and always will be.

Imagine if this life is only one of many and that what is missing now will appear in abundance in the next when it is needed most. Would you still feel cheated? For example, if we are born with amazing treasures such as good health, cherished family, and freedom, and they are unique to this lifetime, we would never know that they are great treasures and unique to this lifetime. We might take those treasures for granted, and if we are consumed with thoughts of what we perceive we don't have, we will miss out on the real treasures that we do have right here, right now. We need to realize and remember that everything is just as perfect as that forest, regardless of where the branches are or their sizes or how they are spaced on any one tree.

I used to wonder, if I suffered a devastating material loss, would I still be okay? And then it happened. Right around 2000, I took out all the cash from my company and invested it in the then-growing stock market in preparation for my retirement. The next day, I suffered a devastating loss; within a few short months, I had lost an entire decade's worth of savings.

On the day I had to sell out to prevent further losses, and for some time after, I was so numbed by sorrow and disbelief that I wished there were a pill that could make me sleep for six months. However, five days after I had sold out, I woke up with a surprisingly vivid realization that neither losing that money nor doubling it would make a difference to my level of serenity or happiness, and I was able to let it go. Not only was I not destroyed by the experience, within a couple of years I was also able to recover—and more. This would not have been possible without my spiritual growth. My Higher Perspective helped me see that even the large amount of money I had lost was insignificant in comparison to what I had. I remained grounded and did not cause real damage to myself through fear and anger, and it was natural that my experience and growth helped me accomplish more in the following two years than I had in the previous ten. ■

Realized Dreams Won't Bring Happiness

You simply get used to all of the stuff.

I SOMETIMES ASK people to articulate what they see as their highest possible level of success and then imagine that they have achieved it. I ask them to meditate over extended periods on what it would be like to wake up day after day with all of the possessions and opportunities they had ever dreamed about. If you do so faithfully, you would understand that ultimately there would be no change in how you feel.

I was fortunate to achieve my dreams of success early in life while I was still in my twenties. This was of value, not because it made me happy but because it made me realize that achievements and acquisitions cannot bring me the happiness I seek. Otherwise, I might have wasted my whole life chasing a mirage, as so many people do.

I had thought that success would bring me happiness because its power would allow me to buy all the things I wanted and give me the freedom to do all the things that I wanted to do, not the things that I had to do. I used to dream of not having to work ever and just enjoying life and hanging out with my friends, meeting great new people, and visiting interesting new places. I thought I would buy the nicest cars, clothes, home, and tech toys. And then I got it all. At first, it felt amazing, and I was so proud that my friends and family knew all about it. Incredible as it may seem, this feeling was short-lived. That magical feeling didn't last, and it didn't keep me from depression or drug abuse.

Most people thought, and would still think, that I was just ungrateful, and that if they had the same fortune it would be different for them. Naturally, every one of us reacts differently to a situation, but if anyone were more appreciative, it would be because of their inherent nature—who they are—and not what they have or have attained.

I discovered that you simply get used to all of the stuff. When you buy a nice car and drive it, after a while you become accustomed to it. You do not feel the same elation that you might have had when you first purchased it. As you buy another and yet another expensive car, having one becomes the norm. When we reach the norm, we feel norm-al! We feel the same as we felt before. I still wanted to become free to do what I wanted and to buy what I wanted, but now the bar was much higher. Wanting never ends. The only way to change this is to no longer think that reaching the next, higher bar brings happiness. Otherwise, one risks losing hope of any happiness.

A few years ago, I was supposed to go to my cousin's place for dinner one evening. It is a forty-five-minute drive from my home. When I got into my car, I realized that I was going to be early. So instead of driving as I normally do, in the left-hand lane at the speed limit plus 15 percent, I moved the car over to the right-hand lane and put it on cruise control at the speed limit minus 10 percent. As I was cruising, I put on one of my favorite songs, "One of These Nights" by the Eagles. What hit me was how incredible it sounded on my nice car stereo. That brought back memories of my younger years when I dreamed of success so that I could afford such quality things, and that is when it hit me: this car and stereo that I dreamed about having and had worked so hard for and was so blessed to own had become something that I hardly ever had a chance to enjoy. If it had not been for the fact that I had miscalculated my arrival at my cousin's place, I would have just sped through to my next destination without ever slowing down to smell the roses or sing along with the Eagles. Material objects—what I thought would be the fruits of my success—had become, in the case of my car, nothing more than mere transportation for me. I would have been much better served if I had learned to enjoy a ride on a bus instead of taking my car for granted. This does not just apply to objects, though. It applies to everything that you might think will bring you happiness and fulfillment if only you attain it—be it money, or a relationship, or a place to live, or a job.

One day, I went to Vancouver to visit my daughter who is an avid skier. I took her to a store and told her that I wanted to buy her new skis and an outfit of her choice for her birthday. She started to jump up and down in joyful excitement. Even the saleswoman from the store joined her. I will never forget my amazement as I thought to myself, "Why is she so surprised? Surely she knows that I could and would buy her anything that she wants at any time?" It was such a beautiful moment. I sat and watched my daughter and the saleswoman and felt an inner glow because my child still had what I seemed to have lost—the ability to be excited about buying something—simply because I had been pretty much able to get whatever I wanted whenever I wanted it for so long. There was more pleasure in buying a gift for someone else and seeing her excitement than in buying anything for myself.

I asked my daughter a while later, "How come you never ask me for money? You know I can help you in many ways." I am happy she never took me for granted but I was starting to wonder if it was because she was uncomfortable asking me for help. She replied, "I don't need it, Daddy. I don't understand why people need money to be happy." Well, that made me feel incredible—I knew that something was amazingly right with her, and that I might have had something to do with that. ■

Happiness Is a Way of Thinking

Only when I step back do I see my blessings and that nothing more that I could ever gain would make a difference. True happiness is a way of thinking and comes from loving just being part of life, and not by adding material things at some imaginary point in the future.

IT IS HARD for most people to relate when someone says that money will not bring happiness. They think, "Oh yeah, it's easy for you to say because you have money." So, instead, let us imagine telling the blind man I saw in Egypt that vision will not bring him happiness. Anyone reading this can only imagine how horrible it is to be blind, so how can you explain to a blind person that someone can see and yet still be unhappy and ungrateful? It is convenient to think that money is different because we can buy our way into or out of anything, but the sad truth is that there's no real difference between having money and having vision: once you have them, they become the new baseline for wanting yet more to make you happy.

It seemed that no matter what I achieved, I just stored it away and took it for granted, and immediately resumed my search for more. I realized eventually that they are all mirages of fulfillment and discovered repeatedly that only when I step back can I see my blessings. Nothing more that I could ever acquire or achieve could possibly make a difference. I discovered that true happiness comes from loving others and yourself—not from adding to a garage or bank account or real estate portfolio at some imaginary point in the future.

Think of how many times you have received something after dreaming about it—a promotion, a new relationship, or a great vacation—and how it soon became clear that none of these things materially changed the way you felt. As I mentioned earlier, I often ask people to articulate their highest level of success and wants, and then to imagine that they have reached that level. Meditate over extended periods on what it would be like to wake up day after day and go about life with all the possessions and opportunities you ever dreamed about. If you do so faithfully, you will get past the initial euphoria and eventually the way you feel will not be any different than before. In reality, it might take a few months, weeks, or even days. If you were inherently restless before, you still will be. If you were not satisfied with what you had, you will not be satisfied with anything you have. You may feel gratitude and appreciation for what you achieved because you know how hard it was to get it, but you will not feel a magical eternal happiness and contentment indefinitely as you might have imagined you would.

I am so aware today that we need a certain level of deprivation to develop a reservoir of excitement so that we can be satisfied. We need to continue to experience some pain and deprivation and wanting in order to continue to feel happiness and pleasure and contentment. In a way, constant gratification is a curse. ■

Challenges Are Guides

The only thing that feels bad about a challenge in life is the feeling itself.

MOST OF US welcome new challenges at work, especially when they are accompanied by a promotion, because they signal someone's confidence in our abilities. Similarly, we feel proud as parents when our child is given added responsibility in school because it shows that our child can handle more challenges. Instinctively, we understand that these are very positive developments. Paradoxically, we have the opposite reaction when they are real-life challenges that affect our personal growth.

Take, for example, the initial sadness I felt when a patch of trees died in a prized area in my backyard. Once I overcame my negative reaction, I transformed the area into an even better and more beautiful one than it would have been had this "disaster" never happened. It now contains better species of trees to complement the ecosystem, along with new elements that instill calm and integration in a manner I'd never hoped for or anticipated.

Challenges force us to correct, to improve, and to grow. More importantly, they are our Higher Power's way of directing our attention to the areas that require immediate attention. It is like a self-monitoring system that tells us when and where we need to change. No matter what the challenge—or even crisis—is, the outcome can and will always be better if we are in the right frame of mind to tackle it. This obviously seems hard, especially in extreme cases where we have suffered great losses, devastation, and death, but even then, if you have a deep-rooted faith in life and the Higher Purpose and Perspective, you'll get through them. ■

You Need to Experience Pain to Feel Happiness

The trick in life is to welcome and even celebrate our challenges as essential opportunities for growth and to reset our "joy dial."

MY SHOWER TEMPERATURE dial froze one day, and when my plumber checked it, he told me that it was because of the calcification of water, which happens when the dial is not turned for a long time. He said the way to avoid this problem is to turn it all the way down to cold and then all the way up to hot a couple of times every month.

This is similar to life: being stagnant results in loss of movement and reduces our range of responses. For example, if we hear a constant hum for a long period, our ears start to tune it out; after a while, the only way we can even tell there is a hum is if it stops. This is because the body works to counteract any deviation from the norm. If we introduce a noise or even a drug that is stimulating, the body suppresses its sensitivity to counteract that change. Conversely, if we supply a depressive drug, the body will work to excite its senses in an effort to counteract that effect. The human body is always working to neutralize or stabilize the effect of environmental factors as best it can to establish a new "Ground Zero" so we're not overwhelmed by constant stimulation or depression and are able to detect small changes from there. We become more sensitive at this new Ground Zero to small changes that might otherwise be drowned out by our over-stimulated senses.

The same is true for all our physical gifts—health, senses, mobility, security, family, and friends. For example, if we experience pain or the loss of a body part such as a front tooth, or we develop severe pain in an arm, or have a cast on our foot, we become so focused on the deficiency but we eventually get used to it. However, once that deficiency is remedied and we are able to smile confidently or stop feeling the pain or are able to walk again, we become happy and grateful for something we took completely for granted before we lost it.

This is also true for our emotions. For example, we are normally shocked by the sight of violence, but if we are subjected to a constant barrage of it, we will develop an increased tolerance to the point that we will not be affected even if we witness extremely violent acts. Conversely, if we feel constantly depressed, eventually we will get used to feeling that way and nothing is likely to depress us further. Consider how when we master a video game level we become far less interested in repeating that experience and look for our next achievement, or how new action movies strive for bigger battles and explosions to capture our attention. The bigger the challenge, the greater the opportunity for growth and fulfillment. Repetition does not bring happiness.

Having everything working at an optimum level for extended periods inevitably becomes our status quo. We have to lose a gift to become fully aware of its importance in our lives and to appreciate it and to allow it to bring us happiness again.

Therefore, as life presents us with ever more challenges, it is important to remember that difficulty is a natural part of growth. First, feeling pain has a positive side in that we will be able to appreciate everything more, and we will receive gratitude and joy from simple things such as having our health, or use of our limbs, or being able to hear; or having our family safe, or a place to sleep, or a purpose. Second, our greatest growth happens when things are bad, because we are forced to address the problem and develop safeguards against encountering that specific problem again, especially if and when we face it with multiple other challenges at the same time.

The expectation must not be to experience happiness continuously or to avoid pain completely, because eventually that stops working and starts hindering our growth. On the other hand, we need not actively seek out pain or loss of happiness, because life presents us with enough challenges to accomplish that. The trick in life is to welcome and even celebrate the challenges that are presented to us as essential opportunities to grow from and to reset what I like to call our "joy dial," or our gratitude and happiness sensitivity. There is no better choice than choosing to be engaged and to do our best, just as we would want our children (or Inner Child) to do rather than miss a life experience altogether.

For me, my greatest frustration with challenges was that they kept me from achieving my goals, but I learned that the problem was in my fixation with achieving "my goals"—that fixation hindered my ability to handle these challenges in the best way possible. Always remember that life works perfectly. ■

Emotional Challenges

When emotions are triggered, logic dissolves and our reactions are dictated by self-centered feelings such as fear and anger rather than by reason.

CHILDREN ARE SENSITIVE because they have not yet developed their inner strength and sense of grounding. If they face rejection and criticism, their self-confidence is easily shaken and they might feel inadequate or unlikeable. Children develop their inner strength through love and attention during their early stages of development. As adults, they become capable of seeing others' needs and reactions as reflections of those people's perceptions, visions, and limitations rather than as a defining statement of their own self-worth. Conversely, children who do not develop their inner strength during childhood grow up to become adults who require continuous affirmation and encouragement throughout their lives to feel good about themselves.

A small fraction of the human population is on either extreme of this spectrum, with about 10 percent having too great a sense of self-worth and 10 percent having too little. Most people have an average sense of self-worth and suffer to one extent or another from pride, insecurity, and self-centered ego. Therefore, there is plenty of room for improvement and greater happiness in every life.

It is important to remember that our intellects may be great, but we can still be compromised or thrown off course when strong self-centered emotions are invoked. We may be intelligent, but our responses change for the worse when our reaction is intertwined with strong self-centered emotions. I'll share a few recent experiences that demonstrate this self-centered emotional handicap.

In the first example, I was feuding with an associate over finances. We were disagreeing as we often did, so I decided that this time it was better to involve an arbitrator. I prepared for the meeting and meditated beforehand to help me stay objective and not get into a fight because of our disagreement. At first, I felt that my associate was antagonistic and I did all I could to stay cool. Even as my associate seemed unreasonable to me, I continued to maintain my composure. Eventually the meeting started to move in my favor, and at that point my associate started to make some allegations that I considered outlandish. No matter how hard I tried, I couldn't help but get angry and defensive. We arrived at a point where I could not stand it anymore and I stood up and declared the meeting over without resolution. I walked out.

Later that evening, I wrote an email to my associate, my lawyer, and the arbitrator. In it, I expressed what I considered my justifiable anger and proceeded to define my boundaries on future dealings because of my associate's "unacceptable behavior." Thank goodness I had the foresight to request feedback from a friend before sending this email, because that helped me realize its potential negative impact—the conflict would escalate with long-term effects. This was the opposite of what I wanted to accomplish. I rewrote the email with more compassion while focusing on the issues instead of the personalities. The outcome was far better than if I had sent my original email and thus gotten my way through confrontation.

In the second example, later that same week, I received a call from a friend who was in a fragile state and needed advice on handling a bad situation with her ex. She told me that he was teaching their child to hate her and was accusing her boyfriend of abusing the child. The child was tormented and acting out at school. I advised her not to allow herself to get angry and further aggravate the situation. I was able to point out that as long as she was in a good place with herself, all would be well. She needed to recognize that her ex might have been acting irrationally out of hurt and that she could compassionately diminish the acrimony for the sake of both her child and herself. In other words, I could not imagine advising her to do what I did in my meeting, which was to storm out and start a war because of perceived wrongdoing.

The question is: Why did I give her the opposite advice from the advice I gave to myself in a similar situation? Who was I lying to—her or me? I realized that I have a good idea of what is right and what is wrong, but when my emotions are involved and triggered all logic goes out the window and my reaction is dictated by my self-centered feelings such as fear and anger, and not by reason.

There is an expression in AA that says, "Your mind is a dangerous place. Do not go in there alone." I can understand this in so many ways, from when I curse at someone driving in the left-hand lane at the speed limit, to when I justify my anger at someone else's wrongdoing. I have learned that no matter the situation, I always need to stop myself from reacting based on my emotions because they will always produce an irrational response and I will always lose!

Every time I have ever asked for someone else's opinion I've been amazed. Whether I did so for an email at work in reaction to an upsetting event or for something far more personal, having an outside opinion helped me take a step back and see the Higher Perspective and a much better way of handling the situation than the emotionally charged/induced reaction that comes so naturally to all of us. Even when I knew in advance that my buttons would be pushed and I had every opportunity to prepare via consultation and meditation, I would still frequently fail at some point.

When it came to the conflict with my business associate, the answer for me would have been to not go to the meeting in the first place. There is nothing wrong with negotiating through a third party. In that case, self-centered emotions would not have been triggered by direct confrontation. It is the ultimate show of self-love to protect ourselves from trigger situations and prevent an emotional downslide that can compromise well-being. I learned to turn the negotiation and resolution over to whatever medium is best suited to a situation, such as lawyers or arbitrators, and to simply accept the outcome, whatever it may be, as the Higher Purpose. In the end, it does not matter what the outcome is, because as I have seen repeatedly, there is no way of telling which outcome is ultimately best for me. ■

A Disease of Perception

Recovering addicts who are forced to seek, and become highly reliant on, their Higher Perspectives can experience a greater serenity and joy in life than those whose self-centered perspective was not nearly as damaged and were therefore not forced to make any improvements.

I ONCE HAD a strange dream that I lived in a village somewhere in Europe during World War II, trying to survive and make the best of things for my family, my friends, and myself until the war ended. There were also three free-spirited women who hung around town and would appear from time to time, always laughing and singing. One day, I was recording something in my room and left my tape recorder on when I had finished. Shortly afterward, the three women entered my room, and I happened to record what they said. They alluded to there being no war and that they had created this alternate reality in our minds. The women laughed at how we could not see it. They were so arrogant and complacent that they would even sing, "there is no war," and laugh as we dismissed their comments as joking around, never once imagining there was any truth to them. They were witches and we were under their spell.

When I woke up, I realized I had had a vivid nightmare. That is when it hit me: my dream was not that far-fetched, because I had experienced such distorted perception in reality. The reason I surrendered to the fact that my life was unmanageable when my addiction was active was that in that glimpse in the mirror, I saw that my addiction possessed my mind and had created an alternate reality. My disease was using my mind to perceive everything in a completely unreal light, causing me unspeakable pain and ultimately causing me to isolate myself and self-destruct through drugs. In other words, it may not be character defects making our instincts imbalanced, but rather our faulty perception causing what may be a perfectly normal reaction to a perceived (un)reality and making the reaction seem irrational, even insane.

Consider the fact that we seem to know what is right and wrong and are capable of rationally advising others on matters that are not pertinent to us, even when we do not or cannot follow our own advice. We must assume that it is a perception problem rather than a processing problem. This is why we are capable of becoming happy and serene when we adopt a Higher Perspective. In this way of looking at our lives and the world, we see things from a different perspective and thereby bypass our faulty self-centered perception.

Faulty self-centered perception never goes away in any of us. It is hard-wired into our brains. Everyone's experiences create a distinct lens that filters their perception in a manner that is as unique to them as their DNA. Further, we do not even realize the differences any more than a color-blind person realizes they cannot see colors as others do without special testing. Any two people will look at the same situation and see things differently to varying degrees. The difference becomes more pronounced the more our ego or self-centeredness is involved. Therefore, the best way to see reality is by having a diverse group of people provide a collective perspective. It is like superimposing several distorted images of the same scene; in the resulting collective image, the elements that are most commonly seen will become more pronounced and the final composite will reflect a truer image than any one person's perspective.

For long-term recovery from addiction, an addict must not just become completely abstinent, but must also find a support system that continuously corrects or even replaces their extreme perception defect. Addicts struggle with the most basic emotions of hurt, anger, resentment, and more throughout their lives, even long after their complete abstinence begins. Finding such Higher Perspectives minimizes the effects of this extreme self-centered myopia.

When I first attended AA meetings, I could not understand it when I would hear someone proclaim that they were grateful to be an alcoholic. Later, I understood. Paradoxically, recovering addicts who are forced to seek and become highly reliant on their Higher Perspective can end up experiencing a greater serenity and joy in life than non-addicts whose self-centered perspective is not nearly as damaged and who have not therefore been forced to make any improvements. It is like someone who relies on a car with common defects and normal breakdowns versus someone who had to abandon their dysfunctional car and now uses public transit that works efficiently and provides far more benefits than any car, let alone an average one, ever could. ■

Life from Different Viewpoints

It is only by letting go of our fears and expectations that we can take life as it comes. Every day presents a fresh blank canvas upon which life paints another masterpiece.

UNFORTUNATELY, I AM one of those people who get easily irritated when they are trapped in the left-hand lane behind a car traveling below the speed limit. The other day I had a dream that I was in such a situation and that it was particularly frustrating. I was in my usual rush, with a car ahead of me driving at what seemed a significantly lower speed than the limit allowed. I could not pass in the right-hand lane because there were sporadic cars that blocked my ability to pass it. However, there were a couple of opportunities when the car in front of me could have moved to the right and allowed me to pass, but did not. I grew furious. I honked and flashed my lights and tailgated to make it clear that I wanted them to move out of my way immediately!

Finally, there was a break in the traffic and the car slowly moved over to the right, at which point I pressed hard on the gas to pass it. As I looked over to express my anger, I was shocked—I saw myself as an old man driving that other car. In my dream, I shifted over to being the old man driving the other car. I realized that I had been trying to move out of the way because I was aware that the person behind me might be irritated just as I used to be when I was young, but my older reflexes were too slow to allow me to do it safely any sooner. As my younger self passed and made a hand gesture and called him names, my older self felt frustrated and embarrassed and called the younger me names. It may have been a dream, but it was a look into my future. It helped me see that life is meant to be experienced from different perspectives so that we can learn as much as possible. Life's unpredictability from infancy to old age presents a myriad of different perspectives, joys, challenges, and opportunities. I will experience life at good times and bad, hungry and full, satisfied and dissatisfied, and so forth; over time I will feel different degrees of gratification, frustration, happiness, sadness, love, abandonment, inclusion, isolation, safety, fear, success, failure, fame, obscurity, leadership, and adherence. How else can one be fulfilled by life's journey? It is only after we look at life from every possible viewpoint that we grow and appreciate life's amazing intricacy, and feel content and ready to move on to our next chapter.

Just as when a tree viewed close up may appear imperfect until we see it as part of the forest as a whole, the difference in that perception is the frame of reference that can only be had by letting go of all fears and desires. I must not revel in previous successes, let alone wallow in past failures, because I cannot separate the good from the bad. Even if I could just hang onto the good, I would still miss the new good. I must shed my goals and aspirations as well as my fears of the unknown. All that I have learned—much of which comes to me intuitively—about projecting success to achieve success ties me down in a self-centered world that separates me from my spiritual perspective and gifts.

If we view our lives from the Higher Perspective, we will become more connected and at peace with it. We will feel more serenity and gratitude, and our fears will diminish. It is only by letting go completely of our fears and expectations from the past or future that we can take life as it comes day by day.

Imagine being divested of everything in the past, both good and bad, and from any expectations, fears, or desires in the future, while being open to what life brings your way. We all know and believe that life will continue to offer us unbelievable gifts and opportunities; by shedding our past and expectations, we would thrive as never before. It is only when I shed even my most treasured fantasies of experiences that I allow myself to see and fully experience new ones with a greater sense of appreciation and gratitude. ■

How Do We Gain a Higher Perspective?

It is only by first letting go absolutely of our self-centeredness that we can begin the journey that will enable us to discover our Higher Perspective.

SOMEONE RECENTLY ASKED me, "How can you believe that everything happens for a reason and that we have no control over anything?" This question immediately reminded me of the way I used to see things. Before my descent, I always felt that, barring a natural disaster, I was in complete control of my destiny. I made my choices and reaped the consequences accordingly. As life threw challenges and opportunities my way, it was up to me to overcome them, seize them, or go in a different direction. I thought I was in control and fully responsible for my actions and hence the consequences. I have changed a lot since then!

The question also reminded me of a documentary about astronauts and space that I once watched. The narrator explained that in the early stages of space exploration everyone was fixated on reaching the moon. We were so consumed with reaching it and seeing what was there that we didn't expect that once we arrived the greatest discovery would be made not by viewing the moon close up but by looking down at the Earth from space. Our planet was breathtaking and awe-inspiring in its beauty, vastness, intricacies, interdependencies, and fragility. It put our world and life in a perspective no human had ever seen before.

This is a perfect analogy for how I gained my Higher Perspective and later my understanding of a Higher Power and Purpose. It was not until I let go of my self-centered perspective and control that I was able to float far enough away from myself to see my world and life from within a completely different frame of reference. It was only then that I realized I am part of something much greater than my immediate surroundings or understanding. I was able to see objectively how I interacted with people and my surroundings and the impact that had on both the way I feel and how others feel about me. I was able to see that the only thing I have real control over is my peace of mind and happiness. I can either go with the flow and enjoy life or fight it and waste the greatest gift any human can ever receive.

We can never gain a Higher Perspective from a self-centered point of view. Therefore, we can neither acquire faith nor count on it to give us a Higher Perspective. By "faith," I mean a belief that we are part of something bigger. It is only by first letting go absolutely of our self-centeredness that we start the journey that will enable us to discover our Higher Perspective and Higher Power (which I'll get into in the next chapter). This is the journey that I had to take. Letting go completely was not easy—the concept of total surrender eluded me. In fact, it was akin to a miracle that I managed it. I would never have given up control if I had had any choice. This was something that I had to do to overcome an addiction that placed me in imminent danger of death.

A psychiatrist once told me that the concept of total surrender was far too simple for me to understand because I was too cerebral, but the longer I explored it the clearer it became.

I imagined being placed on an island full of dangerous terrain, animals, and plants that required my extreme caution and full attention to survive. Eventually I would be stricken with bouts of sicknesses, cold exposure, poisoning, starvation, dehydration, loneliness, anger, and frustration, all to the point where I might be depleted and find myself in danger of dying. Now imagine there was a tour company that developed and refined the ultimate holiday excursion to enjoy all the elements of that island safely and with all the conveniences a person could want. Would it not be great to hop on board a tour bus to take advantage of everything on offer instead of spending all your energy and time trying to navigate and fight the elements? From my perspective, I would then have all the time and luxury to take in the sights, connect with others, and fully enjoy my experience on that island. My special skills and whatever positive innate abilities I had could still be used, but in a way that allowed me to get the most out of my experience.

For many reasons—abandonment, depression, and addiction—I had found myself on my own version of this island. Since a young age, I had felt that no one understood me and had learned that I could only trust myself. Furthermore, as I survived on my own, I developed a lot of strong skills, including endurance. I was able to find shelter and learned what and where to eat and how to survive, even if I was bruised and unhappy. I knew that my skills were special and that not everyone could survive on the same island as long or as well as I could. That is why it was difficult for me to discard everything and completely surrender.

Naturally, all of this talk is in metaphors. In reality, such is the experience of our lifetime on Earth. It applies to our way of dealing with our emotions and perspective on our experiences. We might find refuge in isolation, competition, holding grudges, and drinking. But there is a much better way that results in happiness and a sense of purpose through belonging. As I developed a Higher Perspective, my concept of God or a Higher Power grew into something different from what I was taught early in life. I started to realize that God is life, which has been completely tested and proven to me by all there is across infinite space and time. Through the simplicity and beauty of surrender, we connect to something far greater than we are, and it feels like returning home. ■

3 / Finding Our Higher Power

God is beautiful life itself—
vast across the whole universe
and time. Humankind is just
a minuscule part of it.

A CLOSE FRIEND ONCE TOLD ME THAT he enjoyed my writing, but when it came to the parts where I mentioned God, he was completely turned off and felt shut out completely. He reacted strongly, and understandably so, based on his perception of what God is, which is completely different from what I mean when I use the term. In fact, everyone's belief or understanding of God is not only different, it is as unique as their DNA. It is because of this, and the fact that I can identify strongly with his reaction, that I am starting my chapter about Higher Power with what God means to me.

I spent my youth in a very religious Christian family in a very religious country where almost everyone believed absolutely in God within the context of their religious denomination. It did not matter what religion you practiced as long as you practiced one; those who did not believe in any religion were considered satanic. Nowadays in Egypt there is a sweeping wave of intolerance for any religion other than Islam, and elsewhere in the Middle East even between various denominations of Islam, but it wasn't like that when I lived there.

Growing up, I always feared God to my core. He was an enigma. On one hand, He was all-loving and forgiving; on the other, He was judgmental and mercilessly punishing, all the while having complete control of our attributes and destiny. This left me totally perplexed as to how anybody can be held responsible for any action. Still, I did not dare question God because of the fear that was instilled in me about doubting Him.

When my family immigrated to Canada, I discovered that Christianity and the Bible were interpreted differently on this side of the world. Descriptions of Christ and God and His Will differed from one faction of Christianity to the next and from one century to the next, not to mention from one religion to the next, so I started to question whether my religion was an interpretation of God rather than the absolute timeless truth I had been told to accept.

This realization made me question my religion for the first time ever and opened the floodgates of cynicism in my mind. Moreover, my scientific studies contradicted its religious fundamentals and it started to make no sense to me. Soon I became an atheist. I even developed a deep dislike for my previous interpretation of God, whom I started to view as nonsensical, cruel, and completely unforgiving. I rejected the idea that if I had a "sinful" thought (and it seemed that everything I liked was sinful) I could burn in hell for all eternity.

As a child, I could not imagine how a loving God could burn someone alive, causing them what must be unspeakable pain, and to do so repeatedly forever and ever. What kind of creature, let alone God, would create a hell like that? How could even Satan be any worse? And what kind of a God would allow his "children" to kill one another in His name or choose one race over another or ask yet another race to kill innocent people in His name as if He could not do enough killing Himself? By my late teens I had resigned myself to the belief that my religion served a purpose for the weak and the hopeless with its after-life fairy tales, but it was not for me. This shift in my opinion made me feel empowered, strong, and independent. Little did I know—I had thrown the baby out with the bath water!

In my thirties, when I was going through my dark times of depression and addiction, I was told that I had to connect with the concept of God or a Higher Power for guidance. As I have mentioned, it was only by letting go absolutely of my self-centeredness and doing as my counselors told me—"Fake it until you make it"—that I was able to explore the concept of God in a completely new way, and I started to meditate about how things would be different if an unconditionally loving God existed. For example, I was tormented by the injustice of being betrayed and by thoughts like: How could they get away with it? How dare they after all I did for them? Life is not fair! I cannot rest until I get even!" Suddenly, I felt that my anger and need for vengeance could be taken away because "God" would remove my need to get even and retribution would no longer be my call. This would lift a huge weight from my shoulders. I also thought about my actions and losses and how at times I completely humiliated and discredited myself. I was consumed by shame, anger, remorse, and the need to prove myself. Once again, I thought that if God existed and were all-knowing, I would not need to prove anything. He would already know my good heart, deeds, and intentions. Another weight would be lifted from my shoulders, and so on. Furthermore, I felt that I would be safe because I am His creation and "child," and all I had to do was to follow His guidance.

I started to realize that God is much bigger than I had ever imagined and is in perfect unison with logic, science, and all my instincts and intangible feelings. Now I see God as Beautiful Life itself, vast across the whole universe and time, of which humankind is but a minuscule part in this place and at this time. This is not the "God" I thought of when I believed that God was an entity with a mind that I could comprehend. To me, God is much more than the collective consciousness of all creatures because God includes all life forms, life's creation itself, and infinitely more matter and energies and other places and things than I can ever imagine even to this day.

Sometimes the worst thing that can happen in life is for things to be just okay or just good enough, because then we do not develop the need to search out and perhaps find something much better. This is true of everything, including relationships, careers, jobs, and places to live, and especially true when it comes to finding greater spirituality. I had inadvertently turned my back on God and my Higher Power when I "threw out the baby with the bath water." As I sought new awareness, not only did the weight of my incredible pain start to lift, I unexpectedly developed a new sense of what God is to me. In other words, only because I was seriously searching did I find something much bigger than I had ever anticipated. ■

What Is God?

Being connected to God grounds
me in the universe and frees me to enjoy the
wonder of life as it is meant to be.
The one thing I wish for the people I love is
that they each experience this connection.

REGARDLESS OF YOUR religious orientation and whether you believe in a Supreme Being or intelligent design or a spiritual concept of a Higher Power or complete random processes, we all know that we are part of something much bigger. In this book I use the word "God" to refer to that bigger perspective, but you may substitute it in your mind with the God of your understanding, or with the words Higher Power, Higher Order, Good Orderly Direction, Love, Life, or whatever else you prefer.

There are many religions, all with different interpretations of God and God's Will, and within them there are variations or denominations. For example, within Christianity, there are Catholic, Protestant, and Greek Orthodox, to name but three; in Judaism, there are Orthodox, Conservative, Reform, and Reconstructionist; and in Islam, there are Sunni, Shi'a, Sufi, and Nation of Islam. A Wikipedia entry estimates there are about 4,200 religions, and about 41,000 denominations within Christianity alone. Even within the same denomination, people have different interpretations of God. Moreover, many people do not believe in any religion and have their own understanding of or doubts about what God may or may not be. Sadly, the differences in interpretation of God and God's Will even within the same religion has caused wars, segregation, and ethnic cleansing.

Irrespective of any spiritual awakening I might have had, my personal experience cannot compare to that of countless others who have devoted lifetimes to their understanding of God, and since my own understanding changed drastically over time and continues to evolve, I have developed the utmost respect for everyone's personal needs and for their understanding of God. However, when we consider our tiny place within the vastness of space and time, how can anyone profess an intimate understanding of what God is? I have come to realize that God is unimaginably beyond us and the more narrowly we try to define God, the more mistakes we make and the more out of touch with God and our understanding of God we become. Moreover, while questioning religion may help us to understand our interpretations of God, much too often it is entangled with questioning the existence of God, which is the grave mistake that I made when I "threw out the baby with the bath water."

For me, it was extremely difficult to reconnect with the concept of God or a Higher Power after I had turned my back and lost that connection. I am not even sure if I could or would have ever regained it had it not been for the near-death crisis that I experienced through my addiction. First, I had to surrender completely to erase my ingrained prejudices and determination. Then I had a spiritual awakening that made me see myself simply as a human and part of a beautiful largess. I say simply to emphasize "without all the trimmings that I sought," but in reality, I was awestruck with gratitude and with the magnitude of the infinite beauty of being alive and deeply connected to others. Then I started to see my life from a Higher Perspective through the eyes of other people, and that's when

I came to realize that we are all part of something far greater than I ever imagined, and became comfortable with calling it God or Higher Power.

Being connected to God grounds my core to the universe, and nothing is more powerful than that. This gives me faith that no matter what happens or how things appear, it is all part of something much greater than I can comprehend. This creates peace since I do not have to figure things out or try to control them, because I cannot, and also because I know everything will be okay regardless. I am no longer invested in the outcome but just in the process, and this helps me live in the moment. This also frees me from self-sabotage and allows me to enjoy the wonder of life as it is and as it is meant to be. If I could wish for anything for someone I love, it would be to feel this connection. ■

It Is Not Just Life as We Know It

As I searched for new awareness,
the weight of my incredible pain lifted
and I began to develop a new sense
of what God is. In doing so, I found
something far bigger than I ever imagined.

WE ALL HAVE a basic working knowledge of our physical attributes and to a lesser extent our emotional being, but we know little about our consciousness or soul and probably have no clue about what other dimensions and particles are within us or that we live within. Life is infinite through time and space. Earth is billions of years old, brimming with life in every square inch, from its core and the depth of the seas right through the expanse of the stratosphere. We cannot find anywhere on Earth where life is not present in abundance. Life is looking for an excuse to happen in every form imaginable. Think of how difficult it is to sterilize anything to ensure that unwanted life forms such as viruses do not develop even in minute spaces and under the most onerous conditions.

There is no question in my mind that we will someday find proof of abundant life throughout the universe. Our solar system has one star and a few planets revolving around it, similar to an atom that has a dense nucleus with protons and electrons revolving around it. Is our entire solar system just an atom in another, much larger reality? Space is infinite and could be layered with completely different realities of multiple and interwoven sizes.

One cell in our body might be an entire universe with vast spaces and countless galaxies of molecules, and within them atoms that are each the equivalent of our solar system—or our entire solar system could be a mere atom on a vastly larger scale. Naturally, the physics are different, but that is unimportant. Moreover, all of this is just what we can see or measure with our instruments. Interwoven with all this are countless particles and energies and who knows what else that coexist and are in balance on every scale and in every dimension. Our bodies are made up of things that we cannot begin to imagine, yet we get lost in the illusion that we know enough to deem ourselves the only creature with a "soul" because of what we perceive as our unique intelligent consciousness.

Science shows us that there is no way that anything comes from nothing or becomes nothing. Matter and energy and whatever other forms of being are continuously fluid and intermixed. We know, for example, that our bodies are made of physical matter in the form of molecules and complex configurations of cells, and that all of them are displaced every few years, just as a flower comes into being, withers, and is reabsorbed into the soil, and another flower is created from intermixed parts of previous flowers and other matter. Nothing is ever lost and everything that exists transforms. The whole universe continuously intermixes as it moves both forward and outward. It is not just a linear progression of matter and energy as we understand them—there are countless other forms and dimensions that we have no clue about. We do not even have the slightest idea what we are made of. We have a basic working knowledge of our physical attributes, although less knowledge about our emotional being, but we know little about our conscious being or soul and absolutely no clue about what other dimensions and particles live within us, or that we live within.

Think of our challenge to understand aging or how our DNA predisposes us to certain illnesses; or go beyond our physical being and think of our complete inability to comprehend what our soul or sense of self is or where it comes from or is going to. Similarly, our conscious minds are dreadfully limited in their scope of awareness of what more could be inside us. ■

Life Goes On and On

However incomprehensible it may be at the time or in this lifetime, everything will always turn out for the better.

LIFE GOES ON and on. Some lives are good and some are bad, some easy and some hard, some short and some long, some fortunate and others seemingly unfair. Maybe our existence is meant to be a complete experience of everything (all things that may appear good and bad) through the stages of our enigmatic existence.

How do we know that if someone is wealthy in this lifetime they are not destined to be poor throughout the next—or were not poor in a previous lifetime? Having different blessings and challenges in each life helps us to grow and be more fulfilled than if we just had the same life over and over, good or bad. We feel fulfilled when we grow from experiences that challenge us because we need the resulting knowledge for whatever journey we are destined for (see "You Need to Experience Pain to Feel Happiness," p. 62). The point is, we don't know, but we ought to know that it is the way it is for a much better reason than we are capable of figuring out.

Take, for example, one of the most horrific things that can happen to anyone—the senseless death of a child. Of course, there will be unspeakable pain, and of course, there will be total disbelief and confusion as to why this happened. It was so random, so unnecessary, and so inexplicably horrific. Notwithstanding all that, the soul of that child did not disappear or become nothing any more than it just appeared from nothing.

Nothing of that child is gone. It was always here and always will be. What I call the "particles" that once made up that child were redistributed into our surroundings in the same manner that every one of our particles is redistributed upon our death.

If you have faith in God or a Higher Power, you can take comfort in your belief that the child is never lost. The child's life is a preview of its beautiful existence that remains forever present within us. All the matter and energies and whatever else came together in the form of this child's life always existed and will continue to exist regardless of that child's lifespan. However incomprehensible it may be at the time or in this lifetime, everything will always turn out for the better. There is a better outcome eventually for all, regardless of how we get there. With faith in this everlasting goodness, we are able to continue our lives of progression with love and warmth and serenity and gratitude for that child's presence in our lives, no matter how short, and ultimately accept that we have no capacity to second-guess or question it, let alone be angry and bitter about it.

If we examine our lives honestly, we will invariably regard all stages as crucial to our fulfillment—both the good and the bad. We want our offspring to experience the caress of childhood as well as the hard work necessary to become a whole adult. We want them to learn from their mistakes and struggles and to develop strength and empathy for others, and in the end, to understand and experience real love, happiness, and gratitude. From there it is not such a big leap to consider that perhaps each one of us will exist through a series of lives, each with its own struggles and different stages of growth and development, bringing us ever closer to a fuller and richer existence in this universe or wherever we are meant to go.

No one knows what our ultimate destination is, and regardless of whether we know it or not, would it make any difference to how we live our lives today? Life goes on and on—sometimes good and sometimes bad, sometimes easy and sometimes hard, sometimes short and sometimes long. Maybe life is meant to be a complete experience of everything through the different stages of our enigmatic existence.

Just as there are large gaps and clusters of branches in my earlier example of the Christmas tree, in real life this appears as an uneven and unfair distribution of dearth and excess. If we were to balance them out there could be dire consequences, just as the spacing of branches can affect birds' habitat. Our lives are full of different experiences in which one moment we are happy and then sad, strong and then weak, or even rich and then poor. We already know that hardship can build tolerance and empathy, as well as strength and character. Just as birds may need uneven branches in order to fly and nest, we need varied conditions, circumstances, and experiences in order to grow. These myriad lessons are critical during every lifetime. ■

God's Will

God's Will is another way of saying "life's path." The more I respect God's Will, the more I plug into the Higher Power that created all that exists.

GOD'S WILL IS the path that life intends for each of us and we cannot possibly do better. By seeking God's Will, we can plug into vast, proven wisdom and enjoy the best lives imaginable, or we can squander it by trying futilely to steer it toward whatever direction we imagine would be better. There is no way that even the most brilliant, educated, experienced, or enlightened human being can compare to the infinitely tried, tested, and proven wisdom of life itself. The way life naturally unfolds is perfect, at least when compared to human awareness.

Earth has the right balance of matter and energy for life, which started billions of years ago and continues to evolve. From the first organic molecules and their interactions, every single factor has played a critical role. The properties of atoms, sub-particles, electrical currents, radiation, gravity, magnetism, temperature, mix of elements, Earth's size and rotation around the sun, and the sun's distance and energy, plus countless other factors that we cannot even begin to imagine, must all coexist in perfect harmony. And as new life develops, it also affects the environment and all the other interdependent factors that are woven into the foundation of evolution. Every single mutation that occurred and survived in every species had to coexist with every other factor it encountered. Trillions upon trillions of single-step changes built every life form after every imaginable possibility was tried repeatedly, and only when they passed all possible tests and challenges did they move on.

I once watched a large colony of ants moving debris next to a waterfall that would kill any ant upon contact. I studied them for hours as hundreds upon hundreds died, and then I noticed one ant in particular. It was washed away, but a pebble flipped it onto a leaf that carried it to safety. The leaf became stuck on a dead tree branch that lay over the water and the ant climbed on it and walked all the way back up and halfway across. It reached a pile of sand that crumbled and then it fell onto a dry spot before moving off again. That ant went from one spot to the next with an unbelievable mix of lucky coincidence and moves and somehow miraculously made it to the other side. I wondered what it would be like to watch that ant start this incredible journey from the beginning and follow its every move in perfect timing to end up at that exact spot. It was overwhelming, because there was no way to predict what would happen along the way. That ant did not have to be the strongest or smartest, start from any particular location, or take any particular path. Out of countless possibilities, it just happened to make it.

That is how evolution works—one tiny step at a time and no way to plan it. The vast variety of species on Earth demonstrate that there are countless ways to succeed, but while each tiny step may seem random, long-term development is anything but random. We are the quintessential custom-made life forms for Earth. We cannot survive on any other planet and no other complex alien species can survive on Earth, at least not without a perfectly controlled artificial environment. Everything, including the quantity and lifespan of each species as well as the environment and their impact on it, is in perfect harmony and balance. Complex species survived by using instincts that were custom-developed using the same tested and proven methods. Our emotional and social characteristics are completely predicated on this pattern of evolution. Our love, protectionism, and need for purpose and belonging, as well as our fear, anger, aggression, and revenge, are all part of the natural balance, which has helped us make it thus far.

They say God works in mysterious ways. Consider the Chinese folktale "The Lost Horse," which goes something like this: A man once lived in the northern frontier of China. One day his only horse ran away. Everyone tried to console him, but he said, "Maybe it's a good thing." A few months later, his horse returned with a great stallion and everyone congratulated him, but he said, "Maybe it's a bad thing." His son loved to ride the stallion, but one day he fell and broke his hip. Everyone tried to console him, but he said, "Maybe it's a good thing." A year later war broke out and almost every soldier died in battle; the man's son survived because he could not fight because he was lame. That is how life is and there is no way of telling in advance what will result in good or bad consequences or outcomes.

Our lives mirror the manner in which my ant survived its journey. We could each have infinitely various lives depending on how and where we go, whom we meet, and what we do or encounter. A single split-second decision or move can define an outcome. Even the minutest movement anywhere and anytime could cause a different sperm to fertilize an egg and result in a different being that could change the whole world. It is absurd to think that we can control "the" path that will bring us the most fulfillment and happiness, and it is even more absurd to sacrifice years to get somewhere that we think will make us happy. There is nothing wrong with trying to make our life better if it feels good, but the real treasure is enjoying what we already have right now. They say a bird in the hand is worth ten in the bush, but this is more like ten birds in the hand and they are incomparable to an imaginary bird in the bush. Whatever we pursue could never compare with, and must never be at the expense of, missing what we already have.

So, given the magnificence of all that it has already provided, and irrespective of all the bad we can point to, how can I not trust my Higher Power to take me where it chooses? Trusting my Higher Power allows me to be invested in the process and not the outcome. It is incredibly liberating and uplifting to know that all I have to do is my best and what is right at any given moment and be completely trusting and at peace with whatever the outcome is. No matter what happens, I believe that things always turn out the way they are supposed to, and no matter where I end up, each point is a new beginning full of hope and opportunity. Trusting my Higher Power allows me to live fully in the moment without being distracted by either dwelling on the past or worrying and dreaming about the future. Every new day is a fresh blank canvas, with my Higher Power ready to paint a new masterpiece for me.

How my Higher Power works and how things turn out is what I think of as God's Will. God's Will is another way of saying "life's path." It is what life intends for me, and since I cannot possibly do it any better, then above all else I need to understand God's Will for me so that I can plug into this vast, proven wisdom. The more humble I am, the more I am the quintessential creation. The more I respect God's Will, the more I plug into and reap the benefits of the Higher Power that created all this and me in the first place. I can only do the next right thing and trust God, my Higher Power, to do the rest. ■

When Did You Ever Pay for It Anyway?

To assume that we pay for everything implies that we deserve credit for all our blessings. It does not take much to realize that we never paid for any of our blessings, including life itself.

RECENTLY I WAS driving with my youngest daughter. She said, "Daddy, tonight I want to watch *Despicable Me 2* with you but it is not playing on Netflix." I said, "It's okay, honey, we can rent it on Pay Per View." She answered, "Yes, but I don't want to pay the five bucks," to which I laughed and replied, "Since when did you ever pay for it anyway? Forget what it costs! We'll have a great time together." And we did.

Later that evening I received an email from my office advising me that the Ministry of Labour had ordered my company to pay an outstanding expense item for one of our ex-employees whom we had fired after discovering he had stolen from the company. We did not know how much he had taken until we did an audit, at which point we also discovered that he had grossly inflated his expenses over the previous two years in addition to committing several other thefts.

When I saw the order from the Ministry, I became angry. I responded by advising my staff to appeal the decision and make sure the government understood that this employee was a crook who owed us tens of thousands of dollars and made us lose large contracts as a result of his thefts, and that we had proof of this. Our lawyer responded by saying that we could not challenge the judgment and that we had better pay or we would face penalties and disciplinary action and may even start a whole audit of our expense procedures.

When I read this, I became enraged. Someone not only stole and got away with it, but also was further rewarded by being paid in addition to what he had unfairly received. I had to pay for an expense I had neither sanctioned nor incurred. I wrote back and expressed my rage and ordered that our company procedures must be changed and made much tougher so this type of incident would never happen again. The bottom line, however, was that I was left shaking and may have acted unfairly toward my other, honest employees. My peace of mind was destroyed, leaving me defeated, impotent, and angry.

Later that night I practiced the Inner Child Meditation. My Inner Child was upset about this incident. Being the "parent" and advisor in my meditation, I found myself telling my Inner Child, "We have to let go of it. It isn't worth it. Just as we advise others who face situations outside of their control to let go and let God, no matter how fair or unfair it may be, we too should let go of this." My Inner Child responded, "Yes, but will I still have to pay for it?" And I found myself saying, "Since when did you ever pay for it anyway?"

I could not believe those words came out of my mouth! I realized that just as I provided for my daughter to enjoy the movie and be safe in her life overall, so had my Higher Power provided for me to enjoy my life. After all, God has provided everything and in enough abundance to cover all the costs for us to enjoy life without the worry of those things outside of our control.

To assume that we pay for everything implies that we deserve credit for all our blessings. Yet, it does not take much to realize that we have never paid for any of our blessings, including life itself. The cost is therefore between God and that individual. I should not assume control of my account, and instead should be grateful that God has provided with sufficient abundance such that this—whatever "this" means at any given time—will not affect me in any material way. This understanding is beautifully summed up in Mother Teresa's adaptation of Dr. Kent M. Keith's "Paradoxical Commandments," which she kept on her wall for inspiration:

ANYWAY

People are illogical, unreasonable, and self-centered.

LOVE THEM ANYWAY.

If you do good, people will accuse you of selfish ulterior motives.

DO GOOD ANYWAY.

If you are successful, you will win false friends and true enemies.

SUCCEED ANYWAY.

The good you do will be forgotten tomorrow.

DO GOOD ANYWAY.

Honesty and frankness make you vulnerable.

BE HONEST AND FRANK ANYWAY.

The biggest men and women with the biggest ideas can be shot down by the smallest men and women with the smallest minds.

THINK BIG ANYWAY.

People favor underdogs but follow only top dogs.

FIGHT FOR A FEW UNDERDOGS ANYWAY.

What you spent years building may be destroyed
overnight.

BUILD ANYWAY.

People really need help but may attack you if you do
help them.

HELP PEOPLE ANYWAY.

Give the world the best you have and you'll get kicked
in the teeth.

GIVE THE WORLD THE BEST YOU'VE GOT ANYWAY.

You see, in the final analysis it is between you and God;

IT WAS NEVER BETWEEN YOU AND THEM ANYWAY. ■

Countless Blessings

Instead of asking for more things or success, or even safety or happiness, I should instead be thankful for what I already have and try not to forget it.

I ONCE WATCHED a news program on the aftermath of Typhoon Haiyan, which struck the Philippines with unprecedented force; winds gusting at 235 miles per hour were followed by a surging wall of seawater. In the program, a man from a town in Cebu was sobbing and telling how he lost his grip on his three-year-old daughter when the wall of water hit them. He pointed to where she had lain dead in a corner for the past three days. He went on to say that those who remained had no food and he was starving to death. He did not even have the luxury of mourning, let alone burying, his child. My reaction to this story was one of extreme sorrow and grief. I was also overcome with fear—and with gratitude that I had never experienced anything like that.

When I was a small child, I used to watch in amazement when a chicken was slaughtered and the remaining fowl would go about their business as if nothing had happened or was going to happen to them. They walked over the dying or dead chicken, completely oblivious to the demise of their own kind or their own eventual fate. I could not imagine how they could not feel or do anything about it. When I saw the report on Typhoon Haiyan I was struck by how we are not so different from those chickens. We hear and see news of doom elsewhere, and not only do we go about our lives as if nothing happened, we actually remain ungrateful for what we have and bitter about not having more.

Despite our blessings and fortunes, I find myself continuously seeking more of this and less of that, and in the process I lose the magic of the moment. This very moment when I am not threatened, I'm alive, healthy, among loved ones who are likewise safe and prospering, and dreaming outrageous dreams compared to so much of humanity that lacks the basic necessities of life.

I wondered what I would do if I ever experienced such a loss. What if I lost everything and witnessed the horrible death of my child and had to watch her body decomposing day after day while I was in complete shock and, along with thousands of others, groping for sustenance just to survive the day? Would I scream for help? Would I dare to? The thought that overwhelmed me was that I would be ashamed. After all, I am the guy who complained and screamed for help when I had everything that most people want and much more than they could even dream of in the best of times. I was often thankless, frustrated, depressed, and even angry with God for not giving me more.

That is why I experienced shame. I could imagine God looking at me and saying, "There is the man who cried for help even when he had such abundance." Would anyone ever take my cries for help seriously again?

Today, I find myself questioning what I ask for. Instead of asking for more things, success, or even safety or happiness, I try to be thankful for what I already have and to not forget it. I try to remember my countless blessings, to love myself through humble gratitude, to help others, and most of all, to do the things that keep me grounded. ■

Prayer

Prayer is the most beautiful experience, because that is when you share an intimate moment with God and express gratitude for the gifts of your life.

MOST OF US are blessed with caring families and friends during our lifetimes, but everyone comes into this world alone and leaves it alone. It is a direct arrangement between each one of us and God. Nobody negotiated for this life on our behalf, and nobody is responsible for how we live it. Therefore, while people may help us connect with God or our Higher Power, it is important that we develop and fortify our connection directly.

To ask for more is to be ungrateful, because it implies that we feel God did not give us enough. When you consider that we are part of something much bigger and more beautiful than we can comprehend, how can we ask for more or for change? Imagine if you provided your children with everything they needed, even if they could not see it. Wouldn't you want them to trust you, be happy, and cherish their gifts and not keep asking for more without appreciating what they already had? In other words, if you have to pray for something, then pray not to have what you want but to want what you have.

There is no question that we all need help and guidance throughout our lives, and there is nothing wrong with that—we all need other people. However, here is the distinction: We give thanks to God, but we look to each other for help and guidance in our daily lives. We are here to support one another. It is hard to feel serenity and connection with God if we are consumed with self-centered issues such as resentment, and if we isolate ourselves and do not seek the Higher Perspective and guidance from others. It is therefore important to take responsibility and to nurture our connections and our support structure.

Imagine, for example, that you are a student chef in a kitchen, learning how to prepare something special. Think of God as having provided you with taste buds, the kitchen, utensils, equipment, ingredients, plus everything else you need to learn and to prepare all you want. Then think of your companions in the kitchen as your guides on what to prepare and how to prepare it, including which ingredients to use, what temperature to cook them at, and for how long. In other words, God already made sure that everything is there for you, so isn't it a little too much to also expect God to tell you what to cook and how to cook it and to make sure that it turns out perfectly? How will you learn to be a chef? It would be like doing our children's homework for them. Is that love? How would that help them in the end? God gives us the freedom and ability to make those choices so that we may learn and grow. If it turns out bad, it will taste bad; if we do it right, it will taste good, and we can enjoy it and go learn something new.

Prayer is how we stay consciously in touch with our Higher Power and our blessings. Our relationship with God is direct; it is unique to each of us and so should our prayer be. Write your prayer and memorize it. Be ready to go to that special place with your Higher Power; say your prayer aloud, and improvise if it feels right.

Prayer is the most beautiful experience. It is that time in a day when you share an intimate moment with your Higher

Power and reminisce about the best gifts of your life. God is your absolute best friend and is always there for you no matter what, from the beginning to the end. Just as you would with someone you care deeply about, nurture that relationship and develop the most beautiful setting in your mind wherever you are when you pray. Laugh and smile about the wonder of your life. For example, if you have children, think of how magnificent they are and share by ad libbing about how much love and joy they bring you. Express it in words and thoughts; feel the warmth and appreciation for your blessings from your inner depths. If you do a proper prayer—at least twice a day, morning and night—with strong visualization of the beautiful parts of your life, you will be so excited and impatient to go on with your day and embrace them all.

Here is my first prayer. I wrote it one morning in Biloxi, Mississippi, when I was in awe at nature's beauty and overwhelmed with gratitude:

> I marvel at the vastness and infinite beauty of your universe.
>
> I humbly thank you for giving me life; to share this incredible world and existence with you.
>
> What could I have ever done for you to deserve such a blessing?
>
> Thank you for my senses to hear, see, touch, smell, and taste life.
>
> Thank you for the flowers, the oceans, and your marvelous creatures full of splendor.
>
> Thank you for the company of families and friends giving me an identity, a memory, and a feeling of belonging and purpose.

Thank you for my children, a fruit of love. What more of an honor than a child in my likeness, entrusted to me to love, care for, and shape its life.

And as my children become independent and even distant, I am grateful for the blessing I had during their childhood.

When I do feel unhappy or depressed, I feel gratitude because it reminds me that it is my freedom, power, and responsibility that give me the ability to go anywhere.

As I lose my loved ones, I thank you once again for the most beautiful experiences and the moments that I had the fortune and blessing to share with them.

Thank you for a BRAND NEW DAY.

I love you for all that and for more than I can express.

I love you with all my heart.

Most people believe that prayer is a way to ask for more things, but it is designed so that we can give thanks for all our blessings. ■

The Invisible Father

There are times when God helps us that we will perceive as interference with our plans.

MY DAUGHTER NYLA was excited to show me a video she had watched in school about how small Earth is relative to the Sun, which in turn is tiny compared with other stars. Earth is like a grain of sand next to a mountain when compared with some of the largest galactic bodies. Nyla marveled even more at how our entire galaxy is infinitesimal compared with the universe. I showed her another video—one of our Sun hurtling through space at 43,000 miles per hour and demonstrating how Earth and other planets are not only rotating around themselves and the Sun but also spiraling through space in a vortex at extremely high speed.

My daughter gasped and asked in amazement, "Where are we going, Daddy?" I thought for a moment and then answered, "No one knows, but at least we are all together." I asked her to think of how infinitesimal our lifespans are compared with a billion years—a small fraction of the Sun's journey. We laughed as she recalled a cartoon she'd seen of a fly that lives only for one day, saying, "When I grow up I want to..." and before finishing that sentence the fly had already grown old and died. We are part of something incomprehensibly larger than what is driving our lives. How can anyone believe that they can understand it, much less control it? There is no question in my mind that the root of serenity comes from embracing life on life's terms.

For example, when Nyla returned to school after summer vacation one year, she was devastated to learn that she was in a different class from all of her best friends. The school advised me that they had done this for the girls' benefit since they distracted each other in class. I understood, but that explanation did not sit well with Nyla. She countered with many arguments. I acknowledged that it could have been handled better, but explained that I thought it would end up being the best outcome for her in the long run. Nyla wasn't convinced, but accepted the situation primarily because she had no choice. I believe that our discussion and my listening and empathy made it easier for her to come to terms with it.

This made me think of parenthood, and my continuous guidance for my younger daughter, Nyla, and how her resistance is just part of growing up. I love Nyla and want to protect her as best I can. Some restrictions are crucial for her well-being, but I wondered how different it would be if I were an invisible father. What if I was watching over her, but she was unaware of my presence and couldn't see me or receive an explanation for why I do what I do to protect her? For example, if I knew she was in danger I might interfere with her ability to go somewhere, but she would have no idea I had done so or why. The thing that struck me was that if she were completely unaware that I was protecting her, no matter what I did she would always perceive it as interference with her plans.

This is remarkably similar to how the Higher Power works in our lives. If we are unaware or lack faith that something bigger is guiding us, we continuously experience frustration and anxiety when things do not go our way. In fact, the harder we fight it the greater the chance of our being overwhelmed by defeat and isolation. I remember so many times when I cursed God for not giving me a break or letting things work out the way I had planned them, without ever considering that it was for my own good. With that misplaced anger I proceeded to make matters worse for myself.

Having faith that everything happens for a good reason helps me live in serenity. No matter what happens, how much it interferes with my plans, or how negatively I might perceive it, I make an effort to feel acceptance and pay close attention to why a turn of events might be better for me. This type of trust empowers us and is at the root of true serenity. It makes us feel safe and loved instead of victimized and frustrated. If we do not take other people's behavior personally but as part of a Higher Power's plan, we will grow from our experiences. The real magic happens when our serenity becomes natural as opposed to coming from a conscious effort or being something we have to seek.

When we can accept the guidance of our Higher Power and trust our blessings, we will be more receptive to understanding our Higher Purpose and the means to carry it out. ■

4 / Finding Our Higher Purpose

I do not "own" me. I am "free" to
do as I please, but that does not give
me the right to abuse myself,
just as I have no right to abuse a child
in my care. Instead, I have a cardinal
responsibility to take care of myself and
everything else that I can influence.

AS I BEGAN TO SEE MY LIFE AS A GIFT from God, I was awakened to the realization that it was not mine. Life is a gift, and an amazing one at that. I never earned it. I never even asked for it. I had no say in when or where I would be born, what qualities I would have, or the lessons I must learn, and I have no say in when I will die. I do not "own" me. I have "freedom" to make choices, but that does not give me the right to hurt others or myself.

I was created with specific attributes, in a specific place, at a specific time, and for what is obviously a specific purpose. My Higher Purpose, or God's Will for me, is all that matters. This does not mean that I cannot be happy or work hard to achieve more, because these are all essential to our survival and betterment. However, our ultimate purpose is the overall betterment of life and not just our personal gain, and as we fulfill this purpose, we experience gratification and true happiness in our inner core.

The greatest appreciation and gratitude that I can express for my life is to appreciate and take good care of myself and to fulfill my Higher Purpose. Who am I to second-guess that, or to assume control by saying, "Okay. Thanks, God. I will take it from here and do what I think is best." I can do a lot to fulfill my Higher Purpose, but how can I fix or improve my Higher Purpose when I have not the slightest clue about how to create anything, let alone my complex life and all that surrounds me? ■

Life Shows Us the Way

I always felt that our purpose in life is the ultimate mystery, which only those with the greatest of insights are able to comprehend. However, I discovered that our Higher Purpose could not be any simpler, and we receive our instructions daily.

ONE DAY I was watching a news segment about air traffic controllers. A map showing the number of flights that are in the air at any given moment was displayed. There were so many thousands that all I could see were tiny planes. Every pilot must follow a preapproved flight path that specifies the departure point and the destination, as well as the time and altitudes of each flight. Despite the pilots knowing almost everything there is to know about flying and aviation, none of them are allowed to change any parameter of their flight path based on their personal desire. Even a minute variation in any one of these parameters, right down to being a few seconds late or early, could cause a catastrophe.

This is analogous to navigating our lives, but with infinitely more parameters. There are countless factors at play in life, and it's impossible for anyone to comprehend them all, let alone their interdependencies. Furthermore, unlike these pilots, we are not equipped with a flight plan. We don't know where we came from before we were born or where we go after we die or how long it will take and how or why. We get our instructions as we move through our day-to-day interactions; the feedback we both give and receive on navigating life comes through our likes and dislikes, through the negatives and positives, through feeling good and feeling bad, through obstacles and blocks and opportunities, etc. If we want to tap into our Higher Power and Purpose, it behooves us to listen for and follow these instructions rather than being determined to take control and do it "our way."

Things that might appear negative are actually essential parts of the navigation system that guides us in this life. I should not be any more upset about running into a negative experience than I would be if the fuel gauge on my plane warned me that I was running low on gas in the left wing. My reaction would not be one of, "This plane is so irritating or negative." Instead, I would be grateful that the fuel gauge works so that I can take corrective action in time. Living in the now allows us to focus and to handle what life asks us to do rather than being consumed and distracted by what we want to do. Let me demonstrate by recounting a recent experience I had.

I had a two-week window to finalize my edits of this book, but I was disrupted by a series of what I felt were really annoying events. To start, I had a rare opportunity to spend a few days on the beach in Costa Rica where I expected to meet some friends. They didn't show up and I ended up alone. It was too quiet and boring, and although I made the best of it, I could not help but feel a little resentment and upset about how else and with whom I could have spent that valuable time. When I returned to Toronto, I left my wallet in a taxi and spent hours trying in vain to reach the driver. The following day, my front tooth broke in two just after my dentist's office closed and I was stuck at home for the long weekend until the Tuesday—when I discovered they were closed for another week of summer break. I had to spend almost a full day getting temporary repairs, all the time knowing I would have to have most of this work redone in a few days' time. Then, I had a call from my staff at the office to review an important presentation they were about to make and I became quite upset because they were unprepared. I had to spend considerable time on it, which ruined my chance to work on the book that day too. The next morning I woke up to a barrage of text messages hinting at suicidal thoughts and demanding to speak to me from a friend who was extremely distressed. This really irritated me because I was torn between feelings of sorrow and frustration. I was worried for my friend but I knew that talking to them would take hours and consume me emotionally and that my friend never listened to any advice. These "annoying" events continued until I had a chance to step back and reflect on things through a sorely needed meditation.

Life was telling me that I had done enough with the book—I needed to focus on more important things, no matter my plan. For example, I must have needed that time alone on my vacation for reflection and as a reminder to not let other people down. When I broke my tooth, my Higher Power was telling me that I needed to look after my teeth now. When my staff called to review their presentation, my Higher Power was telling me that they needed more help and guidance than I realized. Lastly, when my friend messaged me, my Higher Power was telling me that I am needed to help someone. In short, whenever I become too consumed by the illusion that I have control over my life, such as being fixated on my plan, I stop living in the moment and become less aware of, let alone able to follow, my life instructions to the best of my abilities.

We don't have to stress about what our Higher Purpose is. Through humility and acceptance of what life presents to us each day, we become well positioned to fulfill our Higher Purpose. When we do the next right thing, meaning unfolds and we are shown the way. There is an old saying that, "God never gives you more than you can handle." If I had kept my mind free I would have had all the time I needed to properly address every one of those perceived "annoyances" and recognize them for what they were—instructions on what to work on next. ■

Distracted Living

Without the distraction of worries or dreams, I become more sensitive and capable of discovering things that would have gone completely unnoticed and unappreciated.

FOR MOST OF my life, I had no idea how much I was losing out. I lived my life the way I drove my car. I could get from one spot to the next without even realizing or remembering how I got there. It was all mechanical. Even when I had to pay close attention to traffic, I would normally just react and then go right back to what I had been daydreaming about. My mind was almost entirely focused on other matters. Rarely was it fully engaged and invested in what was happening to me at any given moment. Sadly, just as distracted driving, such as texting while driving, results in accidents, scrapes, missed turns, and cutting people off, so does living life while distracted and not living fully in the moment. Ironically, even a self-centered preoccupation with goals and plans will result in mistakes and missed opportunities—and some of them will be huge.

Once we see our life from the Higher Perspective and trust our Higher Power, we can stop wondering, worrying, hoping, planning, feeling, anticipating, reflecting, and so on about what happened and what might happen. All of a sudden, a lot of noise in our brain quiets down. For me it felt like most of the noise in my brain just stopped. A sudden hush came into my life—the type of hush you experience after walking out of a very loud place. Quiet... clarity... ah! The beauty of clarity!

All of a sudden, I could see even the minutest things with much more clarity. For example, if a flower or a beautiful butterfly is spotted by a very busy brain, it becomes another image on a sheet bursting with images. Trying to isolate it out from the crowd of images would be like trying to find Waldo. However, with clarity and a calm, clear brain I can see the flower or butterfly much more easily and clearly. I am more sensitive to my surroundings. And since my brain and senses are not being continuously pounded by who knows what, they are more receptive and I become more sensitive and capable of detecting many things that otherwise would have gone completely unnoticed and unappreciated.

Once I felt this in my heart, I seemed to enter a different reality, one where time seems to stand still. Think of a movie where everything is in slow motion except the hero, who can react as fast as always. For me, in this state, life slows down but my mind functions at the same pace, which allows me to focus on a narrower point in time with much greater awareness of everything in detail. This is simply because my mind is not consumed by thoughts from elsewhere, be they in the past or the future or anywhere other than the here and now. My world literally slows down around me and gives me the time and chance to see everything around that otherwise would happen simultaneously and so fast that there is no hope of seeing most of it. This is what I refer to as "distracted living."

Be prepared to find it hard to deal with the sudden quietness, peace, and tranquility. Dealing with multiple thoughts about what happened, will happen, and is happening elsewhere in addition to dealing with the present is like an ADD rush. It is very hard to just stop, even once we believe in our heart that we should. We need to train our minds to keep focusing on the immediate in the same manner we would train to perform better in any sports activity. In "Living Twenty-Four Hours at a Time" (p. 159) I will outline how the benefits of a daily routine help to reprogram our mind in this regard.

Paradoxically, mood-altering drugs are sought when the noise is maddening because they create a crude bubble in which our awareness of reality is greatly diminished, providing sorely needed relief. This is why drugs are sometimes confused with the quest for spirituality. But this is akin to bashing somebody on the head to make them stay in the moment. How can that compare to the splendor of unfettered awareness?

This ability to be totally engaged in what is happening at a given moment is also nurturing my appreciation and gratitude for life. In much the same way as we can develop our appreciation for a food or an activity or a place by focusing on it and investing our time to learn about and savor it, we can likewise increase our enjoyment and appreciation for the many seemingly simple yet priceless things that we already have in our lives. Furthermore, I am doing so much better with what comes my way simply because I am paying attention and feeling good. For example, my increased presence when I am with my daughter is helping me to become closer to her and helping me to understand and guide her and to share with her. The moments now count for so much more than when I was just "doing the time."

Living in the moment also makes life more unpredictable and exciting. It is like reading a book one page at a time instead of trying to read ahead, or like walking and paying attention to our surroundings versus driving a car and being focused on our destination. Every day becomes more engaging, with immediate opportunities for new and exciting things. ■

Collective Conscience

People are the best guides to help us understand what to do next.

I ONCE THOUGHT that my instincts were my guide to my Higher Purpose, but while instincts are certainly important tools, they can be manipulated and misdirected by our minds. We are each blessed with an incredible mind, but it can easily turn into a dangerous weapon. Ego can distort our view of the world, sometimes with fatal consequences, as we see by those who kill in the name of God. Animals are purely instinctual and can seem far more spiritual than we could ever be. Geese on their migratory flights don't stop to re-evaluate their purpose in life or have a smoke or a little drink of cider to make the trip more interesting and pass the time. Nothing can improve their natural state.

Clearly, we humans have a cardinal responsibility to ourselves and to everything else that we can influence. If we don't take care of ourselves, nothing else matters. The success with which we take care of ourselves determines the success with which we take care of everything else. Nothing is more of an oxymoron than the expression, "I sacrifice myself for my children or my family," because if we sacrifice ourselves, we simultaneously sacrifice our contribution to the well-being of those for whom we are sacrificing ourselves. The most valuable gifts from God are not material, and neither are the most valuable gifts we can give to others. Taking care of ourselves is the foundation of our Higher Purpose and should be our top priority.

Our parents and teachers told most of us that all we had to do was eat well, go to bed early, and pay attention in class to be healthy and successful. This meant we had to take care of our physical health and spirit. We can take care of our health by eating well, staying active, and getting a good rest. There is no magic to it—just treat yourself with real love and care in the same way as you would treat your children. In addition, we can take care of our spirits by finding our Higher Perspective in order to become less self-centered and more humble, inclusive, and loving, and by finding our Higher Power to feel peace and gratitude.

Our Higher Perspective and Higher Purpose become clear through our collective conscience. We need daily meaningful exchanges of ideas to help us chart our lives one step at a time. When I am struggling with fear, shame, pain, distress, confusion, happiness, or the need for direction, I listen carefully to what others say because I know it is God speaking to me through them. What I also find to be particularly helpful is to become part of a trusted group of four to five people with similar demographics to me and to meet regularly to dive deep into our personal issues, including matters related to sex and money, or whatever else we may be dealing with. We all see things differently, and our perspectives are particularly influenced when we are invested emotionally. That is why a group of people who are not emotionally involved can help us assess our situation more objectively from multiple angles and provide that much-needed Higher Perspective. It is the ultimate expression of self-love and humility to ask for help and close guidance about God's Will for us through such initiatives. It is with incredible honesty and clarity that we see our Higher Purpose through such collective conscience. ■

The Day I Realized I Was a Good Father

I found myself promising my Inner Child to take care of him as I do my daughter.

I DON'T GET a chance to meditate as often as I did early in my recovery but I'm always glad when I do so. During a recent meditation I hugged my Inner Child and thought about how far we had come and, above all, how positive I feel. I have been in a good place and able to enjoy my days for some time now. Still, I knew there was much that I could do to take better care of myself. I have not been doing many things that I could do better, such as getting adequate sleep.

I started to think of how I always make sure that my youngest daughter gets enough sleep and how that helps her to be full of clarity and positive energy during the day. I also thought about how frequently I talk to her about what she sees and feels, including her fears. On a couple of occasions lately she has grabbed my hand at bedtime and asked me if I could stay with her for a little while longer. I said "of course," and asked if anything was the matter. She told me she was disturbed after stumbling on videos of "real ghosts" on YouTube. I sat next to her and told her there are many logical explanations for the images and in any case, there is nothing to fear since they have never harmed anyone we know. I went on to tell her that she has a beautiful mind that can see and create so much beauty around her, from art to music to fashion to writing, and so on. I told her that her mind is precious and developing and to make sure that she fills it with beautiful and positive thoughts and to leave no room whatsoever for bad thoughts.

As my meditation came to a close, I found myself promising my Inner Child that I will take better care of him just as I do my daughter. That's when I realized that I am a good father and can be better still by taking as good care of myself as I do of my family. ■

Imagine

The joy of doing more.

IMAGINE LIVING A long life and reaching the ripe old age of well over a hundred years old. You are frail but still largely have all your physical abilities and mental faculties. You have seen and learned so much and feel greatly fulfilled overall. You have no acquaintances, friends, or family left— even your youngest child passed away many years ago and you have lived a whole lifetime since. All the faces around you are new—the politicians, the actors, the celebrities, the scientists, even the children and people in your immediate environment. There are new borders, new orders, and new socio-economic realities. Despite all these changes, there are still people with feelings and lives like the one you knew, ready to launch a new era, one that you are soon going to leave with complete contentment and satisfaction.

Now here's my question: If century-old you were able to perform one last act of significance for humankind, what would it be? This is part of your Higher Purpose, and there is no reason why you cannot do it now. Think of the joy this would bring to the world and to you. ■

Interesting Facts about the Brain

The most powerful way to resolve old fears, misunderstandings, and prejudices is to re-engage memories associated with such feelings and process them anew with people who can help you apply a Higher Perspective.

THE BRAIN IS a complex network of neurons that look like microscopic trees. These neurons have stems like a tree trunk with huge branches and roots. They may be long stems with huge branches and roots, or short and stumpy stems with thin branches and roots, and in every shape that you can imagine. Neurons are connected by an extremely intricate configuration of their branches and roots, touching at various points. The branches and roots are dynamic, like trees in the wind, always changing where they touch, and in some places they are stuck together.

Neurons are lined with electrons along the outside layer, and when an off/on event causes an imbalance, the electrons are triggered and an electric charge travels like a tsunami along the stem of the neuron to all its branches and roots. These electrical impulses weaken and die off as they travel, but if they remain strong at the connecting points, they trigger cascades of electrical impulses along other neurons. Each in turn may then trigger other events, such as contractions that result in muscle movement or hormonal excretions.

At any given time, a sizeable portion of our brain is actively firing—mostly in the subconscious, controlling functions such as heartbeat, breath, muscle movement, enzymes, and hormones. A thought at any given instant is the portion of our conscious brain that happens to be firing at that time. If you hold on to a particular thought, the contact points remain connected and gradually adhere. A recurring thought or action would coagulate the connections. In other words, they will stick together in that formation to provide continuous recall like constant foot traffic clearing a major pathway in a forest. This is partly how memories are formed. For example, the last thing you want to do with a negative experience is think about it obsessively, because that makes it a permanent and prominent feature in your everyday thought processes. Conversely, if you have a positive experience, then thinking about it will reinforce it in your mind. This is the great advantage of prayer and meditation: we solidify our awareness of our gifts and our connection to our Higher Perspective, Power, and Purpose.

Much of the conscious part of the brain is dormant with many neural connections that have been configured by our experiences but have decayed over time. Portions of a memory may be intact but not the pathways that allow you to reach and recall it. For example, we may have a memory from our childhood that we have not thought about for years. The neuron connections to this memory eventually break down and erode the pathway to it, causing us to forget the memory. If, one day, we see, smell, or think something that connects in some way to that memory, it can light up that entire area of the brain with whatever is left of that memory by the avalanche-like event I described above.

One of my favorite animated movies is *Ratatouille*. At one point Anton Ego, a food critic brilliantly played by Peter O'Toole, tastes the quintessential ratatouille prepared by

Remy, the illustrious rat chef, and is unexpectedly transported via an entire memory from his childhood, including how his mother cared for him and what he was doing and wearing at the time. His experience was magnified because it plugged him into a once-lost cherished memory, all brought to life by a connecting taste memory.

When a portion of our cerebrum, or thinking part of the brain, is firing, every active thought is connected and influenced by various functions of our brain, including our senses, perceptions, memories, prejudices, and ability to reason. All of these shape the memory that is formed and gets stored away. For example, if we feel negatively about an individual, we will process and store our memory of them along with that negative feeling. Even if we later develop positive feelings about this person, that by itself will not change our stored memories—the negativity stored with those memories will continue to affect our subconscious feelings. The only way that we can counteract the imbedded negative feeling is to reactivate the memory through an active thought process using our current perspective to reseat that memory accordingly.

Even verbalizing an event to someone else will engage this correction without our having to receive any feedback from the listener. The brain will have to access the memory to process it for presentation and that will automatically engage a person's current perspective. We can recall events and feelings from memory, but we must engage our (current) way of thinking to explain them. For example, did you ever find yourself saying, "Wait a minute, now that I am explaining this, it does not make sense"? This is why some forms of psychotherapy involve people talking without any feedback or guidance.

The most powerful way to resolve old fears, misunderstandings, and prejudices is to re-engage old memories associated with such feelings and process them anew with people who can help you apply a Higher Perspective to them. Memories also have tentacles—they influence the formation of subsequent memories. Once a problematic memory has been corrected, its entire related network needs to be processed as well. For example, if someone is traumatized by a childhood memory and a breakthrough happens, they will still need to process a good portion of the subsequent memories that were built with the marred emotions that developed and were reinforced from the original trauma.

When I was much younger, I discovered that I could alter ingrained feelings that persisted even though I knew they were not right and did not wish to experience them. For example, I knew that jealousy was bad and a sign of poor character that would only hurt me, but I still could not help feeling that way at times and even acting on that feeling. However, I discovered that when I discussed it frequently and openly with a different perspective, my feelings changed over a couple of years. Now I realize that my feelings changed because I discussed the majority of my emotive memories from a different perspective and reseated them within a new set of beliefs.

On rare occasions, I will do something that embarrasses me and the last thing I want to do is discuss or share it with anyone. Yet those are the most important times to share, because our ego and self-centeredness have taken over. If I don't share, I will invariably put myself down, feel lousy, and then stop taking proper care of myself—just like admonishing a child for not doing better. I learned that no matter how much my ego hurts,

I must share such events with someone I trust. I am always stunned to discover how negative I can be and the good that always comes out of sharing.

Clearing the wreckage of the past is also essential for establishing a proper foundation for growth. For example, if your house is a complete mess, how effective will cleaning up after yourself be from only this point forward? The house will still be dirty unless you perform a good clean-up before you embark on the next stage. To the extent that our Higher Purpose requires us to take care of ourselves, we need to look at and re-examine our old and new thoughts regularly to "aerate" our brain. This is where caring but frank friends who allow us to air and vet our thoughts can really help us. ■

The Art of Listening

True listening is extremely rare because it requires us to be content and serene. Only in the absence of needs and discomforts do we become rich enough to give of ourselves the total commitment in time and incredible energy that it takes to listen intently.

LISTENING IS THE objective yet engaging exploration of someone else's memories and perspective. In its purest form, it requires our total attention to explore another person's mind in vivid detail without analysis or judgment in any way. It is the completely unselfish act of putting ourselves in another person's mind and totally committing to walk through their thoughts with them and have an intimate knowledge of their reality. You do not want to touch, change, or challenge anything, and you may ask questions only to help you understand them better. True listening is rare, even with the people we love the most, yet it is probably the most loving and unselfish act that you can do for someone. Can you think of the last time that you listened or someone else listened to you that way? Sharing such a deep understanding of a person is the most intimate experience we can have with each other. It is what makes us feel connected. We can be around many people and still be lonely if we feel that no one understands us.

True listening is extremely rare because you need to be rich to be able to do it. That is, rich in the sense that one is content and serene, because only in the absence of needs and discomforts do we become rich enough to give of ourselves the total commitment in time and incredible energy that it takes to listen intently.

Once on vacation, I decided to conduct a little experiment. I decided to resist every need and temptation to express or explain myself and instead to listen carefully to everyone whom I met. When someone shared anything with me, I immediately gave them my undivided attention and asked for further explanation or detail. If they asked me something, I was forthright and answered but then promptly resumed my total focus on them. The result was incredible. I have never felt more generally loved, respected, and gravitated toward in my life. I became the sort of go-to person in the background, with people trusting me, asking me for advice, and happily sharing with me their most intimate feelings. Even when asked for advice, I explored with them what they felt they should do; at the most, I asked minimally suggestive questions where appropriate. One person went so far as to describe me as a genius, although I said practically nothing and certainly nothing to warrant the compliment.

We grow by constantly rearranging our thoughts, taking them out and processing them with the latest information and feelings that we have before storing them again. Just like an organized home or office can improve your living or working conditions, this process helps you feel more serene. Our partner, family, and friends are extremely important in this constant airing of views. Not only do our memories and feelings become aligned, but ideally they become aligned with the Higher Perspective. So, if you want to make someone feel loved, set aside some time and really listen to them. In short, we are entrusted with the overall betterment of life to the best of our ability; taking care of ourselves is the foundation of our Higher Purpose and must be our top priority. ■

My Biggest Hero

We already possess everything
that we need. We just have to take care
of ourselves today, and that includes
being honest and loving toward others.

THE OTHER DAY, I was watching a commercial about a man who was described as an ordinary good man who was not particularly strong, famous, or a big hero, but even so, to his little girl he was a hero. I have two daughters, the younger of whom lives with me. I love taking care of her. There is so much to teach and do to help her grow into a confident and well-rounded individual. She means the world to me, and I mean the same to her. I am her hero, but I don't aspire to being another child's hero. I can experience so much love and gratification just by being with her and being a good daddy for her. My children's love is enough and I have no need for other children's love to feel as good as I could ever feel. Then I look at other parts of my life and wonder why I do not have the same intuitive feeling about everything else. For example, why do I have a desire to be needed, respected, admired, and perceived as successful by as many people as possible?

What my Higher Perspective helped me realize is that just as I am completely fulfilled by and content with my child's love without the need for more children looking up to me, I can be similarly completely fulfilled and content with loving and caring for myself. Just as I am my daughter's biggest hero, I am my own biggest hero. I am her hero because I love her unconditionally, I protect her, I provide for her, and I help her in every way that I can and as no one else ever could. And treating myself in the same way makes me my own hero.

My daughter will grow up and one day will be independent and will not need me to put her into bed and help her to sleep and make sure she eats well and does everything that she needs to do. She will continue to be my loving daughter and best friend, but she will move on and will take care of herself. Conversely, I will always have and need to tend to me. It is a lifelong commitment to take care of yourself and be your own hero. When I look after myself, I am my biggest hero. When I comfort myself, enjoy life, and fulfill my Higher Purpose by taking care of myself, I am my own biggest hero. I do not need any more than that. I already have everything that I need and I only need to take care of myself today.

Just as I do not need to take care of all children, I do not need to take care of all people. That's God's job. In fact, that is the biggest advantage of not being God. That is why we say, "Let go and let God." Today I experience such gratitude from knowing that I have it all and that I always had it all, even when I did not always realize it. That makes me feel safe and complete. ■

5 / A New Way of Life

It is not enough to have knowledge; we must also live on a daily basis in such a manner as to promote and stay in that space of understanding and of Higher Perspective, Power, and Purpose.

IN THIS SECTION, I PROVIDE MY THOUGHTS on ways to develop a lasting connection with your Higher Perspective, Power, and Purpose. It's a path to reaching and sustaining an optimal state of well-being. It is one thing to have a spiritual awakening and another altogether to live in a state of consciousness. It is not enough to have knowledge; we must also live on a daily basis in such a manner as to promote and stay in a space of understanding.

Most self-improvement programs fail because they do not take into consideration human beings' incredible inertia and resistance to change. Here's an example from my own experience: Many months ago, I sprained my shoulder and ended up in extreme pain, unable to lift my left arm. I ignored it, expecting and hoping for it to heal on its own. It did not get better; instead, it kept getting worse. I tried to rub it and massage it, rest it, and avoid any strain, but my shoulder continued to get worse and I continued to put off seeing a doctor. About six months after I injured myself, I woke up in such extreme pain that I could not even use my left arm to turn my alarm clock off. At that point, I had no choice but to go to my doctor. He told me that a simple exercise would fix my shoulder. He gave me instructions for a routine that would take about three minutes and suggested that I do it three times each day. I went home, placed his instructions on my dresser, and did not do the exercises. And yet, I felt relieved that I now had a solution if my pain got bad again. Three days later, I woke up crying from pain. That morning I did the exercise. I did it that evening and the next morning too. This simple effort made a difference and the pain was no longer unbearable, so I stopped doing the routine. The question is, why did I stop when the routine worked? Why did I not continue to do the routine three or even four times a day and why did I not do the same with my right shoulder and all my other joints as a preventative measure?

I knew it would make me feel so much better, yet I stopped.

The story of my shoulder reminded me of my mom asking my dad why he was not fixing something that was ailing him. He responded, "It's okay, I'll live." The point is, we are often not likely to do something that we do not enjoy, no matter how easy it is, unless it is essential or we have no choice in the matter, such as being in absolute agony as in the case of my shoulder. I believe this to be true of spirituality—even when armed with knowledge about what can make us much happier, we are still not likely to take action unless we hit bottom and become so completely miserable that our only option is to do something about it.

We tend to settle for the status quo in most areas of our lives, sustaining a minimum threshold just above severe discomfort. We are capable of so much more and our challenge is not lack of knowledge or resources or even motivation. Our challenge is that we are so consumed with trying to control our life that we have little time and energy left to take care of our most important and basic needs. ■

Do the Next Right Thing

No matter our histories–what carnage may have resulted or opportunities were missed–anyone can turn their circumstances around and use the past to achieve a most beautiful present.

I HAVE FAITH that no matter what happens, things will ultimately be okay. I can make this statement because I completely lost control of my life, yet thanks to my Higher Perspective, Power, and Purpose, I got much better. I saw my life in a completely different light and was able to be happier than before. This was contrary to my belief in the need for control. Today, I believe that no matter our histories—whatever carnage we may have experienced or opportunities we have missed—any one of us can turn their circumstances around and use the past to achieve a most beautiful present. It is only a question of when we start to live differently.

When I used to dabble in the stock market, I would beat myself up when I saw a stock increase three-, four-, or tenfold in value within a short period of time and be mad that I had not invested in it. After all, "I knew it was going to do that! If only I had invested in it..." I would calculate in my mind how much I would have made had I bought the stock near its lowest price and sold it near its highest price. I would go on and on about how much that could have changed my life. I used to think the same way about so many mistakes I made or right moves I did not make, feeling stupid, regretful, and angry with myself. I would tell myself, "I am such a loser!" Nevertheless, the fact is there is always another stock that is about to soar. If

I missed Microsoft then Google was next, then Apple, or Facebook, and others still every day.

Similarly, when I missed that stock investment, did not get that promotion or relationship, or made a huge mistake, I did not miss the only such opportunity that life presented to me. There is always another thing that I could do right that could propel me to the highest heights or give me whatever happiness I could imagine. It is never too late to do the right thing, because opportunities never stop coming. There will always be great opportunities to grow, to fall in love, or to strive for whatever your heart desires. Life presents us with myriad opportunities every single day, almost like a conveyer belt that never stops. We just have to be ready to see and receive them. The only way we can do so is to take care of ourselves by doing the next right thing. In other words, by taking care of ourselves through the principles of the Higher Perspective, Power, and Purpose presented in this book, we are always in the best position to recognize and seize these myriad opportunities as they present themselves.

It does not matter where we begin. You could be the last in line and end up at the front of the line. I've seen countless people from every walk of life who have been completely destroyed and have then redeemed themselves and become even happier and better people than they could have imagined. The world loves recovery and redemption stories because they give us all hope. In my case, not only did I come close to death, but I also almost lost everything, including my family and friends, my business, my self-respect, and the respect of everyone around me. I regained everything—my health, spirit, family, business, and money—and more. And it continues—my family, friends, and even colleagues admire my recovery and seek my advice for themselves and their children.

We can become as successful as we can imagine, whatever our past or emotional situations. Have you heard the saying, "You can turn stubbornness into perseverance"? Stubbornness and perseverance take the same amount of will and energy—they're just applied differently. So, even an emotional handicap can be turned into an emotional advantage in the right context. There's a funny line from the movie *As Good as It Gets*, when Greg Kinnear tries to convince Jack Nicholson to try to win his love back. He tells him, "Don't you realize that one of your greatest assets is your willingness to humiliate yourself?"

The beauty of life is that it is simple. Spirituality is too complex to figure out, but it is easy to follow. Work on yourself using these steps as your road map:

- Take care of your physical body through proper rest, nutrition, activity, and maintenance.
- Nurture your spirituality with the Higher Perspective, Power, and Purpose.
- Enjoy life fully One Day at a Time and always do the next right thing.
- Aspire for betterment but never at the expense of your body, spirit, or doing the next right thing.

As we become healthy, the world embraces us. The world will love us when we love ourselves. We emanate love and beauty that will help everyone. ■

Let It Go

If you're running a business, letting go
and taking each day as it comes is a
sure formula for the company's demise.
What I did not realize is that while I am the boss
of my company and have to do certain things,
I am not the boss of my life and cannot control
my destiny, or other people, places, and things.

AS I MENTIONED earlier, at the beginning of my recovery I was told that the secret to happiness was probably too simple for me to comprehend. I was described as being too intellectual, like a stick figure with a big head that keeps toppling. I could not grasp this. It felt as if I were being told I was smart but would die because I was stupid. In my AA meetings I heard slogans like, "One day at a time," "Easy does it," "Turn it over," "Let it go," and "First things first." I thought these slogans were only important for handling the challenges early in recovery, such as strong cravings; extreme emotions of anger, fear, shame, and remorse; facing the prospect of never being able to drink like a normal person; as well as dealing with the immediate consequences of the destructive behavior associated with alcoholism. I also thought that as the cravings lessened and my feelings were dealt with and my life became more manageable, I would be able to take back some control and plan my life one month at a time and eventually one year at a time or longer. I did not realize that the slogans represented an enduring recipe for a happy life. At the time, this was counterintuitive to me.

However, I run a business, people rely on me, and it's important that I control all aspects of my company. I not only have to anticipate challenges and opportunities, I have to plan for them. I have to manage corporate productivity, employee performance and morale, and everything else that may have an impact on the company's future. Most of all, I must have excellent financial tracking, projection, and reporting to analyze past, current, and future performance. I am good at what I do and successful because of it. In business terms, letting go and taking each day as it comes is a sure formula for corporate demise.

What I did not realize was that while I am the boss at work, I am not the boss of my life. My tendency is to seize control of every situation and manage the outcome. As a result, in my life I was frequently on edge due to fear of or excitement about the future, and these feelings can trigger inappropriate and destructive actions. For example, if I am set on a particular outcome and things do not turn out my way, I will develop anger and anxiety and these will further compromise my situation.

I created my company, but I did not create my life. I must keep a Higher Perspective and be cognizant of a Higher Power to realize my Higher Purpose. This means accepting that I am not in control. No matter how much I try to understand my Higher Power's big plan, I will never understand the whole picture—where the world is going and when or how or why. I must respect that I am part of something much larger and do my best by being true to my Higher Purpose without questioning or attempting to control or change the outcome. It took me many years to learn that life is all about living in the now with acceptance while doing the next right thing and having faith in the outcome. Acting as the boss of my life is akin to an employee in my company acting as his own boss. Sure, employees are empowered with autonomy and authority to do their best work, but every job is aligned within the context of larger corporate objectives. Employees must be team players who further the goals of the company while finding personal growth and satisfaction within that context. However, an employee who has a separate agenda with no respect for a higher corporate authority and objectives will never flourish and must be removed from the company.

In the same manner that a rogue employee is destructive and needs to either conform or be dismissed, or a parent who is behaving in a destructive way toward a child must be removed from that child's life, natural selection in life works to eliminate those with acute perception disorder. It is a deadly disease that must be treated, or the sufferer will become isolated and in extreme cases die.

My experiences made me see clearly how I had suffered for no reason. In fact, my knee-jerk reactions triggered by my emotional swings were the only true threat to a good outcome because I risked losing credibility and diverting attention from problems that always seemed to work themselves out in the end. By turning control over to a Higher Power and letting it go, the outcome was always good no matter what happened, but it is only when I look back at an incident from some future point that this becomes obvious to me.

At every juncture in my life when I felt good and looked back, I saw everything prior that might have appeared to me then as a major loss or challenge and a point of extreme fear and uncertainty as part of a good journey that yielded a better outcome in the end. No matter how bad something had seemed at the time, it subsequently became part of a good journey that brought me to this happy point today where I feel good about my life and myself. If only I had faith at the time.

The lesson is that we should not fear the outcome of something, whatever it may be. We do not need to act impulsively out of fear and anger to avenge or control any given situation. Only when we quiet the noise of panic and control do our actions become constructive. ■

Lessons from the People Who Hurt Us

My experiences with people who hurt me are the best lessons, because I can reflect back on them and understand how I might have behaved similarly in their situation.

WE ARE ALL disappointed when the people we treat with kindness hurt us. Now I realize that these people were sent to help us understand how we have done the same to others and to ourselves, even without necessarily realizing it at the time.

I once did a huge favor for someone who repaid my kindness with hostility. I could not understand how anyone could be so ungracious until I took a Higher Perspective in my meditation. When I analyzed their behavior, I realized that this person had been put in my life to show me how I had done the same thing to God and therefore to myself. God gave me many gifts: life, skills, opportunities, love, and the list goes on. But I felt entitled and credited myself for all my success, abundance, and blessings. I insisted on doing it my way and refused to be humble or to listen to what God might have intended for me. I snatched things and pleasures, citing and believing that one has to "seize the moment" and "make the most of it." In the end, I missed the big picture entirely. The gifts I had were not of my own doing. Even my abilities and opportunities were gifts from God. I had the whole world and instead I chose to run after what I thought was worthwhile, ending up hostile and without any gratitude squandering the real gift and almost killing myself.

Our intimate experiences with people who hurt us are the best lessons we can have, because we can reflect on them and acknowledge the similar ways in which we have behaved. Today I can see that the lessons we learn in life are like an online course—we may proceed at our own pace and repeat each lesson as many times as we require. When we find ourselves frustrated because negative things keep happening, we need to remember that we were the ones who did not learn from a previous experience. We learn and move on—or face the same challenge again. ■

Get Rid of Your Resentments

Getting rid of my resentments is good
for me—it is not simply a matter of acquiescing,
but of getting better for my own sake.

FOR YEARS, I was told that resentments are bad and that in order to be spiritual we must get rid of resentments by praying for those who hurt us and making amends for our part in the situation. I felt that one friend in particular had betrayed me in the most hurtful manner and I could not imagine how I could ever forgive and forget, let alone make amends. If anything, I was consumed by a desire to tell everyone what had happened and even the score. Only then perhaps could I consider making amends and letting go of my resentment!

One day my aunt pointed out that just as we keep our entire house clean in case guests drop by, we must likewise get rid of all our resentments, anger, and hatred completely if we want to welcome God into every part of our hearts. Later that same week, someone else told me that resentment is like taking poison in the hope of hurting the person whom we resent. I must have heard this a thousand times before, but for some reason this time it stuck. I realized that getting rid of my resentments is good for me, not the other person, and that I am not acquiescing anything but merely getting better for my own sake. For the first time, I was willing to make amends to everyone, no matter who they were and what they had done.

Still, I could not imagine how I could make amends to the friend who had hurt me so much, so I decided to do it in baby steps by making the amends in my mind first and seeing what happened next. I stopped thinking and saying anything bad about him. Even when the perfect opportunity arose, I did not say anything derogatory. That was all I could do for a while. A year later, that same aunt asked me, as she had a dozen times before, to a luncheon my friend would be attending. In the past I would have reacted angrily and refused, but all of a sudden I realized that I did not feel any anger. I went to that luncheon and was cordial, which was something that I had never imagined I would ever be able to do.

A while later, I shared this experience with my private support group. Someone said to me, "Charles, you have a disease that made you want to kill yourself. Why can't you think of that friend as having a disease that made him hurt the people who loved him?" I was stunned by that. Herein lies compassion. Once again, the power of Higher Perspective allowed me to step back from my self-centered view and emotional entanglement and see the situation from another angle altogether.

The amazing part is that I was able to get rid of the anger and resolve everything that had happened in my mind by realizing that the whole experience was part of a sickness—mine included. In other words, once you realize that you need to make amends for your own sake but feel incapable of doing so directly, start by making amends in your mind in the way you think and talk (or do not talk) about that person. If you do so faithfully, you will find that your anger will steadily diminish. It will then also become much easier to see that person from a different perspective and eventually engage them directly. In my case, this different perspective even made the details of what had happened completely irrelevant. ■

Trust

If we believe in Higher Perspective and Power, then our trust will be unshaken and we will live a fuller and happier life of Higher Purpose.

IF WE REALIZE that we are not the center of the universe we can trust everyone, because our expectation will be that everything is exactly the way it is meant to be.

I sometimes ask myself, "Am I trustworthy?" Of course, I would like to think I am, and I genuinely believe that I am one of the most loyal and trustworthy individuals that I know. However, does that make me trustworthy? It all depends on our definition of trust. Last week, a friend of mine wanted to see me. I had agreed to meet, but as the date grew closer, I did not feel like it. I was not up to it. I had had an exhausting couple of days, and as soon as I allowed myself to think about the possibility of not meeting, I started to fantasize about how I would use the time to rest and catch up on things. As it happened, I did not hear from my friend on time. When I eventually received his message half an hour late, I used that delay as an excuse to not meet. Am I untrustworthy?

We human beings are not perfect. Even if we were, there is no way that we can avoid ever hurting anyone who has any sort of expectations of us. It is only a matter of time before circumstances become such that even our most dedicated allies will disappoint us by failing to live up to our expectations.

When my younger daughter was nine, I asked her what trust meant. She answered, "Trust is never lying to someone."

I asked her whom she trusted the most, and she said, "You, Mommy, and my best friend." I then asked, "How much do you trust me?" and she waved her hand as if to suggest so/so. I asked in surprise, "Really? Just so/so?" to which she answered, "Well, 80 percent... no, 90 percent."

I was surprised, and maybe even a little hurt. After all, there is nothing I would not do for my little girl. I love her endlessly and would protect her with my life anytime anywhere. So how could she feel that way? I asked her, "You don't trust me completely?" and she answered, "Well, it's because sometimes you don't keep your promises." The strange part is that I did not see trust in the same light as she saw it. In fact, when I thought about it further, we most probably all have a different understanding of trust. In other words, I expected her to trust me fully because "when push comes to shove" I believed I would never let her down, but her view of trust is that I should always meet her expectations, no matter what.

This led me to wondering if I trusted myself. I did an Inner Child Meditation and asked my Inner Child the same question: "Do you trust me?" He waved his hand the same way my daughter did! He was right—I had let myself down and far more frequently and seriously than I had ever let my daughter down. How many times did I promise myself to take better care of myself, or to take it easy, or to stop eating junk food or drink too much, or to exercise, or to do better in life, or to be happy? I could continue. It became quite obvious that if trust means to always do what you promise, as well as what is expected, then there is no way I could trust myself.

There is an old saying: "Love people; trust God." Let us go a step further and talk about God in the religious sense. Has

God always come through the way we expect? How many times have we prayed to God and not got what we prayed for? We are constantly reminded that, "God works in mysterious ways," because often we do not even understand God, let alone see Him do exactly as we hope. So, how can anyone trust God at all, let alone completely, if trust means not being hurt or disappointed based on our expectations?

In the end, it all depends on how we measure trust. If we base it on expectation, then it is safe to say that we cannot trust anyone, including God and ourselves. If we do not trust, we will not open ourselves up because of fear of getting hurt and we will live a smaller and less fulfilling or joyful life. If, on the other hand, we believe in the Higher Perspective and Power, then our trust will be unshaken and we will live a fuller and happier life of Higher Purpose. This is because no matter what happens, we will know in our heart that there is a good reason for what happens and ultimately a better outcome for us and everyone else, no matter how it seems or feels at the time. ■

Capitalize on Your Lows

If you ever find yourself completely down and out or even hospitalized or incarcerated, this may be your greatest opportunity to discover and connect with your Higher Perspective, Power, and Purpose in a more meaningful way than would otherwise be possible.

MY DAD ALWAYS told me, "Every cloud has a silver lining." Well, I am here to tell you that he was right! Even when hope is in short supply and we have lost most of what mattered to us, or even if we have lost it all, there is a silver lining lurking behind that cloud.

Most of us have heard the story about the professor who brought a jar, rocks, pebbles, sand, and water to his classroom. First, he placed as many of the large rocks as he could fit into the jar. When he could no longer add any more large rocks, he added the pebbles, which found their way between the rocks. When he could add no more, he poured in sand, which filled up all the spaces between the rocks and pebbles. Finally, he added water and that filled all the remaining space. At the end, he asked his students what they had observed from this little demonstration. Someone shouted, "There is always room for more!" The professor said, "No, the lesson is that unless you fit in the large rocks first, you will never be able to fit them later."

Such is the case with our major priorities. If we do not make room for the large things first, we will never be able to fit them into our daily lives later. However, the professor started with an empty jar and it was easy to allocate room for the large rocks. How can we do the same when our lives are already busy and full? Starting anew after losing it all when we hit bottom is like the professor starting with an empty jar, and that is the "silver lining"! When we start fresh, we get an empty jar, a new beginning, and can do our life right from the bottom up.

When I shared the Inner Child Meditation, I described a profound bond and intimacy that I developed with myself that could have only happened in my hour of greatest suffering and loneliness. Throughout this book, I have described how my defeat and surrender allowed me to discover that I am just a human being and that nothing is greater than being human. I discovered that I am not alone; I am part of something much larger. I have faith that no matter what happens, I will be okay.

Love and respect for ourselves, as well as a faith in life, are the most important rocks, the ones we must fit first in our jar. A crisis that leads to surrender is the greatest opportunity to integrate them into your life. ■

Know When to Push and When to Quit

Sometimes we need help to differentiate between healthy confidence and commitment and the kind of stubbornness that hurts us by making us waste other opportunities.

IN SCHOOL, I became good at scoring high on tests. One critical rule for maximizing my score was to recognize and not waste time on the most difficult questions. It was best to go through the whole test and answer the easy questions first, and then to make a second pass for the more difficult ones. However, even on that second or third pass, it is important not to become bogged down by any one extremely challenging question. The reason for this is that you will waste time that is better invested in solving and scoring on questions that are easier to answer.

The same is true in life. When a task is inordinately difficult, sometimes we have to recognize that it is better to move on, otherwise we will miss the opportunities that life keeps presenting. However, it is not easy to know if or when to quit something that is meaningful to us. A particularly difficult challenge could be a great opportunity, or a sign that we are not following the path that life intends for us. The difficulty in deciding when to bow out is compounded when we consider that our perspective on the importance of a particular opportunity may be skewed in the first place.

As I've mentioned, I faced some hard times early on while building my business. Sometimes I felt that I was crossing a lake alone and that fog set in, so I could no longer see the other side. Were these signs to quit or to persevere no matter how difficult things became and to rise above the rest and achieve huge success? What made the difference for me was that I had absolute faith that I would reach the other side. I could not see it but I knew it was there and that I would make it, even as my fear set in. In this case, I achieved great business success.

On the other hand, when I struggled with addiction I vowed to beat it, just as I had persevered in battling every challenge in my life until then. No matter what anyone told me, I would think, "They don't understand what I am capable of—just look at how I succeeded with my business! Why should I listen to them now?" In this case, my determination nearly killed me and it took a miracle for me to survive my addiction, but how was I supposed to know the difference?

Later still, after my recovery, I faced the extremely challenging task of rebuilding my company to save it after the severe damage caused by my lack of direction and the scavenging of my customers and equipment during my absence. I was advised to let the company go or I might relapse. I found myself once again alone, torn between my determination and belief in myself, and fear of not listening to the counselors who had helped save my life. In this case, I worked practically day and night to save it but I also dedicated myself even more to recovery and maintained very close contact with the people and resources that could protect and help me. The result was that not only did I save my business, but I also experienced much greater success than before.

So there you have it! Determination is a two-edged sword—it helps us succeed, but can also make us fail miserably. How can we tell the difference between healthy confidence and commitment and the kind of stubbornness that wastes other opportunities—the kind that almost killed me as I fought my addiction? These are the most important junctures in our lives, where we need a "private support group" to help us figure things out and see things with greater clarity. Private support groups, counseling, and Twelve-Step meetings are three methods I value for help in knowing when to push and when to quit.

PRIVATE SUPPORT GROUPS

Of particular importance to maintaining our Higher Perspective on the next right thing to do is a private support group to help us resolve important issues on a day-to-day basis. You are probably familiar with the expression, "God speaks to you through other people." We need other people to help us see our issues from a Higher Perspective and decide on the next right thing to do. We may be wondering about a career opportunity or a relationship issue, or we may be struggling with depression, or maybe we just want a second opinion on a decision from someone we feel comfortable with. A small group of trusted like-minded individuals who understand us will benefit us immeasurably with the valuable perspective that they can add by their collective conscience.

Everyone in the group should give and receive equally. Ideally, the group should comprise around four to six people and meet every three to four weeks for three to four hours. You want the feedback to be objective; you do not want to waste any time on idle chat about sports or the weather or irrelevant news. This will allow for in-depth discussions of two or three topics per session. The needs of different participants will vary from one meeting to the next. Over time, trust will develop and a good flow of effective and priceless guidance on everyday issues will evolve.

These meetings were so powerful for me at times that I experienced great awakenings, like when I saw another person's betrayal as their handicap and I could once again love that person and forgive them. Another time, I was complaining about things not going my way. I was frustrated about having put a great deal of effort into something that was not working out no matter how hard I tried. Someone in the group said to me, "Charles, picture God presiding over 7 billion people, each with their own struggles and prayers for help, then think of how your blessings are in the top 1 percent of that population. Yet you stand at the top of your mountain screaming at God, 'What about me?'" This humbled me tremendously. It became another milestone in my spiritual growth and I have reflected on it ever since.

To start such a group, first look to identify trustworthy candidates of similar demographics and qualities that you admire, but who are not close friends or family. Solicit their participation by sending them a brief note proposing its benefits, structure, and formation. You will be surprised by how receptive people are and how many others they might recommend.

COUNSELING

In "Interesting Facts about the Brain" (p. 123), I discussed how memories of our experiences are stored intact with our feelings and perspective at the time the memories were created, and that we need to bring them out and reprocess them with a different perspective if we want to modify them. Such modification can result after someone has experienced a change in their perspective, such as through therapy or, in the case of childhood experiences, simply reaching adulthood.

Naturally, counselors can help immensely in the retrieval and reprocessing of such memories, but my added suggestion here is to incorporate the magic of private support groups. This is because the power of multiple perspectives can help not only the individual but also all the participants. The role of the counselor in such group discussions is one of facilitation to help promote trust and focus the group on issues of general or particular importance to the participants.

TWELVE-STEP MEETINGS

Alcoholics Anonymous meetings are referred to as AA meetings. Other Twelve-Step meetings relate to groups like Narcotics Anonymous, Cocaine Anonymous, Gamblers Anonymous, Sex Addicts Anonymous, and Overeaters Anonymous. The meetings provide an invaluable support structure for people with a substance or behavioral dependence. However, Twelve-Step–style group discussions can be extremely beneficial for people in general, not just addicts or alcoholics. Magic happens in these rooms where people communicate with humility in a manner not found elsewhere in society.

The anonymous nature of the meetings provides a safe environment for sharing personal thoughts. Even being in a group of people who are not part of our daily life provides a safer or more comfortable setting in which to share thoughts that are otherwise hard or even impossible to share with anyone we know. These cannot replace the private support groups discussed earlier, as those are intended for deep diving into specific topics with the intent of cross-talk and guidance.

Twelve-Step groups are generally larger, often without cross-talk or even any need to talk at all, and occur at various times for regular participation or spontaneous participation whenever the need arises.

I value the sanctuary Twelve-Step meetings provide for sharing my personal experiences and emotions. They give me "time out" from my daily routine that I can spend with like-minded people. I get the chance to reflect on what I said and did or feel about things that are happening in my life right then, and this helps me to take corrective action. Often I verbalize little thoughts to give me greater transparency. All this greatly enhances my ability to view my life from a Higher Perspective in a regular and timely manner. ■

6 / Living Twenty-Four Hours at a Time

I learned that the meaning
of life is to live, to be invested
fully in the moment.

ONE OF THE MOST IMPORTANT WAYS to make sustained changes is to live your life twenty-four hours at a time and incorporate the changes into your daily routine. I saw a program on CNN in which the author of a new book argued that being healthy is less about eating the right foods and vitamins and more about eating the same things in the same quantities at the same time every day. This is because we can better manage what we eat—a routine helps the body optimize the ways it processes foods and repairs itself. You may think that grabbing an apple or a banana instead of your usual food choice is good because fruit is a healthy option, but the change might actually wreak havoc on your system. In other words, it is best to eat the same foods every day and at roughly the same time.

This makes a lot of sense, and we can see how the same principle applies to all aspects of our lives—physical, spiritual, emotional, social, and intellectual. It would be ideal to start and end each day doing roughly the same things at the same time and for the same duration.

Human, and even animal, evolution is based on having the same routine every single day with minimal change. At the beginning of time and for centuries afterward, people lived their entire lives within a small community where everything remained relatively stable for generations. The routine was set largely by geography, and people ate the same local foods and did the same things for generations upon generations. Even when there were significant changes such as environmental catastrophes or deaths, a new routine was immediately established. History tells us that we are ideally suited for a pattern of routines.

It is only within the most recent minute fraction of our evolution that technology has changed things so suddenly and drastically for us. It is not that people cannot adapt to change, as evidenced by the incredible developments in recent history, but it is natural to expect that our new tumultuous environment would cause widespread anxiety, to say the least. As a result, anything that we can do to bring back as much routine as possible to our lives would be of great benefit. ■

Benefits of a Daily Routine

Sometimes we do not have the ability to standardize or structure our daily routine, either because of responsibilities or simply because we enjoy the freedom of being unstructured. Nevertheless, it is good to remember that there are significant benefits to having a structured routine.

I THEREFORE STARTED to plan my daily routine and soon began to realize that there were more benefits than I'd first imagined. For example, I set aside two hours every morning for writing. I was always stressed about not writing and one evening I was overcome by anxiety that I could not afford to lounge around as I was doing at the time. Then it struck me that I already had adequate time allocated for writing every morning, and suddenly I felt an unfamiliar relief that allowed me to relax and enjoy the moment. Similarly, on another day, I could not write in my allocated time and thought, "Was I wrong to assume that I can follow my routine?" Once again, I found myself thinking, "I have every morning forever allocated to writing, so what's the big deal if I do not feel like writing today or the next?"

These two experiences helped me realize how doing the same thing every day yields serenity in unexpected ways. I am sure this serenity will not only endure but also grow over time in ways that I cannot even predict. Here are some of the most important benefits I've found from having a set daily routine that focuses on doing the same thing at the same time and for the same duration every day:

- It is much easier to master one schedule than to manage our time and activities. Our routine becomes second nature and easy to follow and we are far less likely to infringe on or compromise any priorities.
- We can live in the moment. When we do not worry about things at other times, we are able to focus on what we are doing now because everything that matters is already accounted for and has its proper time allocation.
- Having a detailed routine engages our mind fully in the moment and this helps us from wandering back into distracted living and thinking of other things.
- We will be able to live to the fullest every day by incorporating all that is significant, as guided by our prayer of thanks for all our most valued gifts. You will be stunned at how much time, money, and energy is wasted and what you will save with proper planning. You will effectively add years of fulfillment to your life.
- We can spend each day as if it is our last. We will not fear death without complete fulfillment because each day will be the day. This will add significantly to our sense of joy and serenity.
- We can make changes or additions to our schedule, such as a new relationship, more easily while preserving and not compromising those times and events that are key to our personal grounding.
- A stable and predictable daily routine is intrinsic to human nature. It will provide significant serenity that endures and grows over time. We can deviate but then go right back to our schedule, always knowing where to pick up and what to do every hour of every day. ■

Establish Your Priorities

IT IS A lot easier to set your priorities and manage life one day at a time. Yet, unless we focus on what we need to do and respect every hour and every minute of every day, we can easily waste an entire life one day at a time. Make your physical self, spirituality, and "one-day-at-a time" outlook your top priorities.

PHYSICAL

Taking care of our physical bodies is probably our highest priority. This can be broken down into three main areas: rest, nutrition, and activity. Here's how I did it.

With respect to rest, nothing can be more important than a good night's sleep. This was my priority. I thought carefully about when to go to sleep and how much time I needed before and after to perform my routine, including hygiene, prayer, and meditation before and after bed. Most people do not realize the importance of sleep for detoxifying and repairing the body. Many people spend so much money and time on diets and supplements and anti-aging products, yet sleep is the magic pill and the closest thing to the fountain of youth that you will ever get. Furthermore, sleep brings one of the most beautiful natural highs. Having a good ritual to prepare your body and mind for sleep is paramount. Then, create the perfect setting by investing in a comfortable bed and everything else that you need to enjoy your sleep to the fullest, from your pillows to the lighting in your bedroom.

When it comes to nutrition, a routine will help your body's digestive cycle work at its best and allow you to control your intake of calories and nutrients at optimal predefined amounts and intervals. There are many guides, coaches, and professionals who can help you understand what to eat. It's important to invest time in studying nutrition and creating a healthy nutritional routine and in conducting routine checkups to determine if supplementation with minerals and vitamins is required. In addition, taste is one of our most enjoyable senses, and a carefully crafted routine can give us wonderful moments by allowing us to experience hunger and then satiation. Combining food preparation and eating with spending time with friends and family is a great way to do both and save time.

Regarding activities, you need to incorporate as much movement as possible throughout the day in a way that works for you. For example, you could combine your social activities with physical activity by playing sports like tennis, live in a home with lots of stairs or a pool, choose a career or job that requires constant movement, work outdoors, or walk everywhere you can. Whatever your circumstance, make sure that you get in as much movement as possible without exhausting yourself.

SPIRITUALITY

The priorities for spirituality are at the heart of this book: Higher Perspective, Power, and Purpose.

To keep a Higher Perspective we need to maintain our humility and faith that everything will turn out for the best. To maintain our Higher Perspective, we incorporate our daily Inner Child Meditation, spiritual or Twelve-Step meetings, and as much meaningful interaction with people as possible throughout the day. Scheduling my spiritual time is pivotal. I allocate one hour at noon each day for spiritual interaction with people such as through an AA meeting. I could not find a good AA meeting on Mondays, so I scheduled my once-a-week meeting with my counselor then. If necessary, combine three to four activities into one slot on the weekend to meet or have dinner with family and friends, and perhaps use that same time slot once a month or more to participate in a private support group.

With respect to the Higher Power, we need to write a prayer, as I discussed earlier, and allocate at least three ten- to fifteen-minute time slots a day for prayer. I think one of the most entrancing qualities of Islam is that it calls for prayer five times a day. Try praying to your Higher Power three, four, or five times a day to heighten your awareness and gratitude for your gifts and serenity.

With respect to the Higher Purpose, we need to incorporate our service—self-care and contribution to society—with our career in our daily structure. With respect to giving and helping, it is a good idea to allocate a time slot for spiritual meetings (noon in my case) to volunteer for people who do not have what you have. This will be rewarding in itself, but will also help you remember and increase your gratitude for the gifts that you have and may take for granted— health, security, family, and love, for example.

LIVE LIFE TO THE FULLEST, ONE DAY AT A TIME

With respect to our gifts, we need only look at what we listed in our prayers of gratitude and make sure that we enjoy every one of them, every day. You can use my sample prayer as a guide and see how I expressed gratitude for my life, senses, children, family and friends, and purpose, as well as nature, animals, and plants. We need to allocate a time slot during the day to enjoy and appreciate the sun, plants, and water, and another at night to appreciate the moon and stars. It is important to enjoy the gifts of sight, touch, hearing, smell, and taste.

Simple planning can help us maximize our joy, whether it is savoring taste or smell, listening to music, looking at art, interacting with nature, or enjoying the feel of warm water or intimacy. With respect to family, friends, and people in general, we incorporate our gratitude for these daily. We need to touch family and close friends every day in some way. For example, we might schedule lunch or dinner with one family member once a week or daily with different friends or family members to let us connect with them all. ■

Structuring Your Daily Routine

The challenge in structuring your daily routine is finding the perfect balance between making use of every minute to fulfill your life without leaving gaps for wasteful activities or being too rigid. It takes practice.

REMEMBER THESE SLOGANS:

Live one day at a time.
Live each day as if it is your last.
Seize the moment.
Yesterday is history, tomorrow is a mystery, and today is a gift, hence it is called the present.
The objective is to live our life to the fullest every day.

When we apply these truths, we learn to stop the activities that do not enhance our lives. You will be amazed at how much nonsense and counterproductive activities fill our days, and how we can purge them by allocating all our time instead for what is important. For example, assume our entire lifespan can be condensed into one day, and assume for the purpose of this exercise that our lifespan is one hundred years. This means that twenty-four hours represents one hundred years and each hour represents roughly four years of our lives.

Now, think about spending an hour texting, commuting, watching a TV show, or doing a crossword puzzle. You are effectively allocating four years of your life to that activity. It may not seem like much when you look at it one hour at a time, but over a lifespan it translates into an incredible cost. It is even more alarming when you consider that this hour is robbing you of the most fruitful time of your life. After we have slept for eight hours and done chores like cleaning and commuting for, say, another four hours, and then worked eight hours, what's left? I might average only four or five discretionary hours for leisure and my Higher Purpose. Wasting one hour out of just four or five hours a day is equivalent to wasting a fifth or a quarter of your entire discretionary lifetime. Who wants to waste even one minute on anything that is not truly meaningful?

Be particularly mindful of the time spent online, because it is as far away as one can get from living in the moment. These websites are designed to have you flip quickly from one page to the next. Developers are remunerated by how fast and on how many links you click. It is as unnatural as it gets. We are seduced through manipulation of our biological response mechanism, which was designed for a completely different purpose than flipping through as many pages as possible as quickly as possible, happily forfeiting our lives for some worthless statistical score.

You must protect yourself from such seduction. For example, consider a moth, whose perfectly natural and sound attraction to light is used to kill it. Conversely, consider children and adolescents, whose natural curiosity and impressionability are virtues but in the wrong setting can be harmful. The answer would not be to kill their critically healthy tendency to be curious but to protect them from the misuse of this curiosity. Likewise, you must protect yourself from being seduced by wasteful occupations.

If you fear losing connection by not being online, remember that this is akin to a drug addict fearing they will lose happiness or a sense of inclusion by not drinking or using—the very thing that causes them harm. Staying away from social media will paradoxically bring us closer to the people we want to get close to. Let's find another way to bring us this bird's eye view of what is going on in a time-controlled manner; if we cannot control it, then not having an account might be the only practical choice.

When structuring my day I pay special attention to limiting all time-wasting activities such as commuting and preparation between events. I structure my outside activities for which I have to commute in proper sequence so that I can transition efficiently from one to the next, both physically and mentally. All this may be too arduous to plan daily, but if you do it once for a master plan you will reap the cumulative benefits forever.

Start by allocating time for what is important. Add these anchor items one at a time until you become comfortable with that routine and then add another. I started by anchoring my schedule with my sleep and pre- and post-sleep times and my daily spiritual meeting at noon. Before I retired from full-time work, my work was my anchor. After a month, I realized that I was most ready to write in the morning, and I created a beautiful clear spot every day that I protect. I scheduled 9:30-10:00 as a buffer and 10:00-11:30 for writing. If I was ready by 9:30 and did not need my buffer, I started writing then and got an extra half hour.

I scheduled my writing and yoga after my meditation and spiritual meetings so that I had a head start with my mental preparation. Moreover, I reduced all my commutes by preselecting and sequencing them in the same manner a courier company might sequence its deliveries, each within fifteen minutes by car, which saved me about an hour a day. Then I discovered that I could walk the same distance in about thirty minutes. This meant that I could exercise for one hour by walking to my destination and back and it only cost me thirty minutes more than the time it would have taken to drive. I also saved on gas and parking, helped the environment, and gained bonus time to think and to interact with my surroundings. Just these few initiatives allowed me to incorporate my exercise and more activities within my day and brought me a step closer to living my whole life in twenty-four hours.

Another important time-saving strategy is to superimpose activities wherever possible. For example, combine exercise with commuting and socializing, or if you have children, overlay your entertainment, sports, and hobby time with theirs. Suppose you want to take music lessons and your child does too, then schedule their lesson at the hour that you have allocated to music or hobbies every day. One day you can practice while they take their lesson, the next they practice while you have your lesson, and on other days when you are alone, you may do a related activity at that same hour. You become conditioned to doing this activity alone or perhaps with your children, and may develop techniques that are more effective, whether they are time-saving techniques or mental preparation to minimize distractions. There are activities that we cannot or do not want to do every day but perhaps weekly, monthly, or even less frequently, such as vacations or family dinners. We can still allocate the same time for that same type of activity even if the exact event is different. For example, if you sometimes have a family dinner on some or all Friday evenings, allocate that same time slot to other family activities on other Fridays or during the week, such as parenting or social get-togethers with friends and siblings.

The weekend is a challenge if your routine is different from weekdays. Only vary your schedule where you have no choice, but keep all other routines the same for both the weekend and weekdays. For example, if you work during the week but not on the weekend, allocate that same time to separate activities on the weekend but keep all the other activities on the same schedule. If you have to work an extra four hours one week, try to work each one at the same time every day. If your work schedule changes all the time, do your utmost to change jobs, for it is too expensive on your system—seize the first opportunity to do so that comes your way.

Within this framework, you can explore and further develop each area through the abundance of material and expert advice available. All we have to do next is live one day at a time and watch the rewards unfold. Moreover, as we do we will flourish with an abundance of energy and passion to pursue and accomplish more for our community and ourselves. ■

7 / Spirituality versus Progress

We must not always trust unquestioningly that every new direction or idea that society pushes us toward is the best path forward.

DINOSAURS ROAMED EARTH FOR 65 million years and perished only because of something outside of their control. Sharks have been in perfect harmony with their environment for more than 100 million years! Humans, on the other hand, were not even around a million years ago. We are a new species in this little place called Earth, nestled in a small corner of the galaxy, during a short segment of eternity.

Humans are unique in the way we use our brains. For example, I am not aware of any animal that tries to change its long-term destiny. The furthest planning that I am aware of in the animal world is seasonal, such as gathering food for the winter, and even that is driven by instincts rather than cognitive thought processes. Humans are capable of incredible accomplishments even though most of our inventions simply mimic nature. We observe how a life form or a physical element behaves and we copy it for another use and call it an invention. For example, night-vision technology is based on mimicking nocturnal animals' natural ability to see other spectrums of light. Rocket propulsion is based on containing and targeting the release of energy from atoms that naturally occur throughout the universe. Discoveries in genetics are based on removing one gene after another to see what happens, and then adding them back for a desired effect. In all cases we simply study, copy, and select to achieve a new outcome, but we never create anything like new matter or new laws of physics.

Even so, these inventions have caused gross imbalances in our environment because they are not tried and proven over millennia, as are all natural phenomena. For example, when we transport an indigenous species from one ecosystem to another we disturb the natural balance. This transporting can destroy the new environment, as we have seen with many plants, fish, and animal species. Whenever we disturb the natural balance, there are consequences. The more significant the disturbance, the more unpredictable and far-reaching those consequences will be—think of global warming and massive changes in population and extinctions of species. Incidentally, all of these will result in cascading effects, and what I find particularly disconcerting is the potential for many new species and diseases to appear simultaneously and against which we have no immunity or cure because we had no prior exposure.

Most humans, unlike animals, are also prejudiced to one extent or another against anything and everything that is not like them, whether the difference is color, shape, age, religion, gender orientation, socioeconomic status, power, or dis/ability. I am also not aware of any other animal that tortures another creature or makes it subservient. Animals kill mostly for food, but humans often kill for sport and pleasure. Humans are often cruel to animals and exploit them and other humans for their selfish gain. It seems that the human "higher intelligence" has given rise to something quite sinister as well. I believe this has to do with a self-centered perspective that distances and separates us from spirituality. I have always thought that it is as if our brains overdeveloped during a cycle of evolution and then we were suddenly left with an excess cerebral capacity without the maturity to manage it. Kind of like a child being given a gun—a powerful tool that can be both useful and extremely dangerous, depending on who is holding it.

There are many examples of cultures devastated by new diseases because they have not developed immunity to them and do not have the methods to treat and manage pandemics. I believe it is the same with the ego or self-centered part of the brain that goes beyond the spiritual part. It is very powerful and distinguishes us from other animals, and we have the urge to use it and take full advantage of it in any way possible. Unfortunately, we developed the power to destroy the planet well before we developed the wisdom or maturity to be responsible with this power and for our actions.

The world's economies are not based on a spiritual foundation of connection and sense of love and respect for everyone. The result is that we are hurting ourselves and others by our own self-centered perceptions that make us feel righteous and entitled to reach beyond our natural scope. For example, the other day I walked through a supermarket and was dismayed at the sight of every sort of creature from all corners of this planet, sliced and diced and packaged in almost every way imaginable. When did we develop this need to consume so much quantity and variety? And when did we develop the need to travel halfway around the globe just to relax, or to have multiple homes and TVs and cars and yet still need more and more and more? Sure, it is nice—I'll be the first to admit that— but at what cost? Look at what we are doing to Earth. The status quo is unsustainable and the damage to our ecosystem already is beyond comprehension, and yet we continue to race mindlessly in the same direction.

People can reach their natural capacity for happiness without any of the modern day conveniences—they did so for millennia—and so I am bewildered whenever politicians choose to sacrifice the environment for faster economic growth. What are we racing toward? What is the point of material gain if the cost is unsustainable and still does not bring real happiness?

We must not always trust unquestioningly that every new direction or idea that society pushes us toward is the best path forward. Every day we are being seduced into believing that we must be young, sexy, skinny, rich, extreme, and plugged into everything, and that we must use drugs for instant gratification or to fix ailments, whether genuine or concocted. We can—we need—to continue to strive for betterment, but not without a solid spiritual foundation. ■

Spirituality versus Personal Success

It is natural and healthy to be ambitious and successful provided it is not at the expense of losing touch with your Higher Purpose and the joy of life.

THE JOY OF success is a normal feeling, but much too often we miss the big picture and the real purpose for achievement. Can there be true spirituality while seeking personal success like recognition, love, and wealth?

Many great teachers proclaim that we must be completely devoid of material wealth to be spiritual. While money and stuff may not make us happy, they do not necessarily make us unhappy either. Sure, the more we gain the more there is to lose and this worry sabotages spirituality. This is why many people conclude that it is best to either not mix material wealth with spirituality or not have any material wealth at all. In my opinion, this is a compromise and not a solution, because it ignores a natural need. It is natural and healthy to be ambitious and to work toward personal achievements, provided these pursuits do not cause us to lose touch with our Higher Perspective, Power, and Purpose, and the joy of life.

It is often said that the best things in life are free. We know that our lives and all our priceless gifts of family, friends, and health are worth more than all the money in the world, so is it not wise to do everything we can to protect our investment? Having a great spiritual awareness far outweighs anything that personal success can provide. We would be far wiser to focus on and learn how to fully enjoy our amazing gifts that God already gave us rather than squander our lives in pursuit of a mirage.

Earlier in this book, I wrote about how I had forgotten what I worked for and how my exceptional car became mere transportation rather than the amazing fruit of a success for which I made considerable sacrifices. I am forever reminding myself to slow down and smell the roses, to enjoy what I have earned. If I need to teach myself to enjoy the material things that I worked so hard for and paid so much for, what about all the priceless gifts that I received and take for granted? Does it not make much more sense to stop and smell those roses—the ones that are worth more than all the money in the world?

What can you buy with the second billion dollars that you cannot buy with the first billion? Most people would answer that a billion dollars would be nice enough, but do any of us need any wealth at all to find more happiness and meaning in our life than most people, wealthy or not, ever will? Just look around you and you will see that the happiest people are not necessarily those with a lot of money or fame or power. Where happier people tend to be more successful, it is because others gravitate toward their inner glow, which made them happier and more successful in the first place. In other words, happiness begets success, not the other way around.

I learned that I could enjoy a $10 meal as much as a $100 meal. Sure, it is nice to eat something special occasionally but that enjoyment will not last if you eat it all the time. It is also nice to splurge, but only occasionally because you will get used to it. Take anyone with an expensive taste who would not "be caught dead eating cheap stuff," take the "good stuff" away from them, let them get hungry for a day or two, and then watch how much they enjoy the food. In other words, it is a matter of learning how to appreciate things. No amount of money can replace or do this for us. ■

Charting a Successful Path: Vision, Synergy, and Momentum

No goals are mutually exclusive and you can "have it all" by stepping back far enough to chart your path in life. You'll see that all the paths overlap and you can simultaneously achieve every one of your goals.

WE OFTEN LEARN our biggest lessons from our biggest failures, but success and the resulting accolades tell us when we have done something right. My most significant successes include spiritual growth and recovery from addiction. However, as I've mentioned, I have also experienced many career successes. I charted a successful path early in my life and acquired key skills as a young adult, and my ensuing career success led to significant recognition and financial reward.

Most people short-change themselves by choosing a career just because they like something or because they feel they are good with certain people or situations. It is important to like what you do and to be good at it, but that is just the first step. To be successful you need to be knowledgeable in your chosen field and able to win people's trust. You also need to be in a field that is of great value to many people with strong demand for its products and services such that it offers great rewards to those who fulfill that demand. Lastly, you need to do all this while following a path that is optimally aligned with all your other personal goals. For example, I chose to develop my communication skills in IT because it also offered great rewards.

Someone once told me he did not understand why his father never achieved significant financial success even though he was extremely smart, honest, and determined, and worked hard all of his life. My answer was that it takes more than that to achieve great financial success. It takes Vision, Synergy, and Momentum.

VISION

Identify your passion and vision for the path that you choose.

Some people want to be rich and/or famous, and/or loved, and/or to love their work, and/or to make a difference, and/or to work with animals or children, and/or to travel a lot, etc. No goals are mutually exclusive and you can have it all provided you chart the right path, one that is inclusive of all your goals. Having a vision for your path is crucial, because it lays the foundation for achieving all your goals.

No matter what your passion is, look for a related area that is of high value to society and offers an ideal opportunity to achieve all your goals. It may not be obvious at first but there is always a way. For example, if you love working with children, do not just take the first available opportunity such as volunteer work in a daycare. Sure, you will get the immediate gratification of working with children but it could also be an unnecessary sacrifice. If you have other goals, look for all the ways you can work with children—sports, clothing, counseling, teaching, toys, amusement, and entertainment, for example—so that you can work with children and achieve all your other goals. You should be able to find an area that capitalizes on your unique strengths and maximizes your returns while you pursue your passions. For example, when I chose to develop my communications skills, I searched for a leading organization to learn from, one that was also in a growth industry with significant monetary potential because that was also important to me.

Moreover, things work out more easily when we are on a clear path because life constantly presents us with opportunities that we miss if we are not positioned for them. For example, suppose someone offers you a free first-class ticket to Europe but you must use it in twenty-four hours—chances are you will not be able to go because you will be caught off guard and probably have obligations. Conversely, someone who has been waiting to go to Europe might jump on such an opportunity. People standing on the sidelines might say, "What a lucky guy, he gets all the breaks." In reality, opportunities happen all the time but they only look like breaks when they are seized. The trick is to be in a position where you can take advantage of as many of them as early as possible to take you toward your goal; hence the expression, "You make your luck."

Also, be careful not to invest too much time in a particular path or career that is not progressing steadily because you "hope" that one day you will make it big. Sure, a few win big at the casino, but do you want to gamble with your future? There is always a way to progress steadily on solid ground and get to where you want to go rather than just waiting and hoping for your "big break." If you do not see it, look for it. If you still cannot see it, get help before giving up.

Lastly, never underestimate the value of the environment. The single-most important decision we make is where we settle geographically, for it can complement and bring out the best in us or it can conflict with us and bring out the worst. We can live happily almost anywhere, but we can start by placing ourselves in areas that are most complementary to our personal nature. For example, I felt that being in a warm climate with a progressive environment would make me more active and healthy and inspire me with examples of success all around me. Naturally, this is not easy to do, especially later in life after we develop roots, but it is important to be aware of and to seize the opportunity if one arises.

SYNERGY

Synergy is optimal when your investments in time and energy in all areas of your life are complementary and strengthen one another.

We have finite time and energy and must make the most effective use of them, so make sure to take as many actions as possible to achieve your goal. For example, I switched to a sales and marketing career because it was synergetic to develop my communications skills that I needed for my spiritual pursuits and Higher Purpose, which is to help motivate and inspire people.

Conversely, it is extremely important not to grab opportunities that do not lead directly to your end goal, no matter how tempting they may be. I was offered profitable business opportunities, but I turned them down because they were not in line with my business plan. While tempting, such random opportunities would have only distracted me and diluted my effectiveness. Someone once shared with me his strategy to ensure success: Start ten businesses, because one of them is bound to succeed. I see this as the perfect formula to ensure failure.

Let me stress here that it is more important to know what is wrong than what is right. In other words, you should know what not to say, what not to eat, what not to pursue, what not to think about, who not to date or befriend. Life continuously presents great opportunities. The most important thing that we need to do is to not destroy or compromise those opportunities by saying or doing the wrong thing or being preoccupied by unfavorable pursuits.

MOMENTUM

Momentum builds up when many factors work together over a period to help you travel great distances toward a specific goal.

The next most important factor is momentum. Think of life's accomplishments as the distance a train travels. It takes time for a long heavy train to build speed and momentum and to travel a great distance. Significant accomplishments, including wealth, are built mostly by making steady progress in a given direction over an extended period and rarely by quick giant gains. Therefore, you have to start early, and the last thing you want to do is to lose steam or stop and change direction. Yet, I witness so many people wasting their formative years changing from one career or passion to another and ending up going in circles. Change is important because it is healthy for the brain to refresh its way of thinking and to learn new things, but you must stay the course long enough to build professional status with substantial expertise, credibility, and wealth.

Incidentally, this stop/go and changing of direction is the most crippling feature of our Western style of politics. There is so much to develop and yet all chances of long-term momentum are systematically destroyed as power oscillates between opposing parties working in different directions. Of course, it is crucial to have a democratic process, but surely we can separate long-term goals from short-sighted election campaigns and objectives. For example, a cross-party consortium whose members are individually appointed without causing sudden changes to strategy could handle long-term planning for education and infrastructure. ■

Career Success

The foundation of success and even happiness in all facets of life, including business, is to always pursue our Higher Purpose by having a genuine respect and care for others. Be true to the world and the world will reward you handsomely.

ONCE I DECIDED on my path and switched my academic focus accordingly, my next step was to optimize my opportunities and further my education and training by joining a leading organization in a growth industry within my chosen field. That helped me to develop high-level skills in a real-life environment and to understand the topography of the industry from a bird's eye view. As a result, I was able to develop my expertise, credibility, and contacts as well as identify significant areas of opportunity to eventually go into business for myself. No matter how large an organization becomes, it cannot do it all—and it is not a good strategy to do it all. Even monopolies rely on business partners to supplement their offerings, and I have many colleagues who became successful doing just that.

Once I positioned myself with total commitment and passion in a large area of opportunity, all I had to do was deliver the best I could in an honest and professional manner. I cannot stress this enough: the foundation of success and even happiness in all facets of life, including business, is to always pursue our Higher Purpose by having a genuine respect and care for others.

For significant success, you cannot just act honorably and fairly; you must care about what you do to the depths of your being. No matter how well anyone presents themselves, they cannot completely conceal their core nature. Hence the expression, "You can fool some of the people all of the time, and all of the people some of the time, but you never fool all of the people all of the time." Even people who cannot see it can still sense it and may express this feeling as, "I don't know why, but I don't feel comfortable with that person."

True leaders need only two qualities: to be experts in the field, and to genuinely care for the people around them. Genuinely caring for others is primarily for our own benefit, just like removing resentment toward others, even when it seems counterintuitive. This level of empathy is something that I had to develop further once I came to this important realization. I viewed my managers, colleagues, customers, employees, vendors, and friends all in the same genuine caring manner. I would sometimes meditate before meetings to refocus my genuine care for them (and for myself as one of them, albeit with a higher degree of responsibility). This meant that I had to provide true value with honesty, and that in turn meant that I had to know my stuff to be able to help them significantly to warrant the level of success that I desired.

I witnessed many people cheat or lie or pull "a fast one," and then think they had won—only to ultimately fail and be dismissed by all who cross their path. There are no quick fixes or magic wands. Be true to the world, keep your Higher Perspective, Power, and Purpose in sight, and the world will reward you handsomely. Your ability to relate to and communicate with people is the quality that will catapult you to great success or lead to miserable failure in life.

I have encountered people from all lifestyles and vantage points—when I was poor and rich, credible and dismissed, powerful and weak, loved and hated, admired and pitied, envied and resented. In doing so, I have learned several valuable things.

PEOPLE

People are all different. I used to think that if any two people were presented with the exact same situations, opportunities, and abilities, they would make the same "obvious" choices. I found out the hard way that this is not true at all. Furthermore, no matter how long and intimately you may know someone, if things change in an unprecedented manner there is no way to predict how they will behave. In other words, do not make yourself vulnerable by expecting people to behave in a certain way when things change. These are not intended as negative views of people, just a better understanding. For example, you may love birds but this does not mean that you would let them poo all over your furniture.

People in general cannot predict what you are capable of, no matter how effectively you communicate your vision or how clear it might be. Do not be discouraged if no one around you feels that you can succeed or make it big. History is filled with examples of professionals who did not recognize incredible talent in people who later became extremely successful. One day, shortly after I bought my first office building, I took a colleague to see it. When he walked in, he looked around as he raised his arms in the air, belched a huge laugh, and asked me, "Did you ever in your wildest dreams expect to own something like this?" I was dumfounded because I thought, "Does he not realize that I could have years ago, and that I already have the ability for much more and potential for more still?" It was a real revelation that people believe only in what they can see and touch and not anything that could be described as a potential. If you are capable of great things, almost no one will believe it until you actually achieve those things.

People's highest priority is their personal needs. Always respect their needs and realize that the best way to get them to help you is by helping them to achieve their goals first. Whether they are employees, colleagues, customers, or suppliers, always be mindful of their personal goals, make sure they are aligned with yours, and you will have extremely productive and committed partners.

People need to feel independent and dignified. One of the biggest mistakes that I ever made in business was to overpay some people by a large margin because I believed it would ensure their loyalty and minimize jealousy. Instead, they were the first to turn against me and cause considerable damage when I was vulnerable. I realized later that they became dependent on their high level of earnings and were unable to stand up to me because they couldn't afford to walk out if they wanted to and so felt controlled and resented me deeply for it. My most loyal employees were the ones I treated with care and respect and paid fairly for their position plus no more than between 10 and 20 percent. This is not true only of money; it applies anytime you provide anything of substantial impact to someone who could not possibly acquire it on their own.

People are considered adults by about the age of twenty, but I found out that their personalities continue to go through significant changes and are not substantially developed until about the age of thirty. This is why many couples seem to "grow apart," when in fact they have just matured into who they were meant to be. Now I understand the importance of choosing the family and not just the individual at a young age because it provides insight into their future development.

COMMUNICATION

The two most important rules for effective communication are to establish credibility early and to place yourself in the other person's shoes as often as possible. If your acquaintances and even best friends cannot comprehend, let alone believe, in your visions, how can you expect strangers to do so, especially in a suspicious setting such as a sales call or negotiation meeting or job interview? You need to show what you have actually accomplished in a powerful, clear, concise, and relevant manner.

Throughout my career, I always solicited testimonials. Even early in my career, I used to help my colleagues, and when they thanked me for it, I always asked them to put it in writing and made sure they understood how important it was for me and how much I appreciated it. After delivering a service, I always called my customers to thank them and ask if they needed anything more because I want to receive the best testimonial they ever gave anyone, and I followed up and even helped them write it if they had no time.

Whenever anything went wrong, I always welcomed it as an opportunity for a great testimonial, and probably more sales, because I conducted myself in a professional, reliable manner and not only remedied the problem as quickly as possible but also took steps to ensure the problem didn't occur again. Testimonials are not only crucial to establishing your credibility, they also capture the enthusiasm of the moment, which fades with time.

Regardless of credibility, if you want to make a significant change to someone else's view you must start from where they are, give them an incentive to change, and then walk them through the change. This will enable you to be sympathetic and true to their needs and in turn help them feel secure and committed to the change. If you see little value to the person, be considerate to them and to yourself and move on. We have all heard the cliché of a great salesperson being someone who can "sell ice to Eskimos," yet nothing could be further from the truth. A great salesperson is someone who cares about their client and can identify a great market opportunity for which they can deliver significant value. Reaching prospects and making sales is only part of it.

ENTREPRENEURIAL TIP

If you start your own business, be mindful of positioning, synergy, and momentum. Carefully select a market opportunity where you have a clear competitive advantage and that is worthy of the long-term investment that you will have to make. Also, make sure that all your products and services are synergetic to your target market. For example, I targeted users of a particular computer platform and I never steered away from that. As I expanded, I only added products that attached to that platform, regardless of who made them. I bought, sold, rented, serviced, and supported everything that fit on that platform, and I never bought, sold, rented, serviced, or supported anything that did not fit.

For example, if you want to sell men's shoes, then sell and service all related products such as laces, inserts, cleaning supplies, socks, and storage containers. Bundle them, perhaps by providing a cleaning kit or one free resoling at cost with every purchase. Do not sell or expand into unrelated product lines such as food or housewares or clothing, even if you get a great bargain opportunity. The idea is to make sure that everything you do helps everything else. For example, if they like your shoe restoration then they will bring their other shoes, and because they are back in your store, you are likely to sell more shoes, laces, and cleaning supplies, all because of the initial shoe sale.

CAUTION

When it comes to career success, there are some cautions I'd like to offer.

First, never invest significantly in someone else's dream. There are countless factors that determine success in any business opportunity and are completely impossible to foresee. Even if these factors were aligned, it is equally impossible to predict who can make it happen. The most common mistake that destroys businesses is making a leap-of-faith investment for some potential new market without testing it one step at a time. I financed several smaller ventures for people whom I cared about, and despite my experience and help, most failed miserably.

Second, and related to the above, never mix money or business with friends and family. I cannot even begin to list the number of times that people asked me to help them financially with everything from a pair of shoes to medical bills. All such pleas were extremely sincere, often desperate, and with absolute promises of repayment. Almost no one ever repaid me, and many came back for more, until I finally had to say no, which made me seem like the bad guy. I lost more friends than

I care to count because of their reluctance to face me afterward. Even when they got the money they invariably still needed it for other things far more than they believed I did and so justified keeping it indefinitely. In short, if you want to help someone, make sure you have purely altruistic motives, do it with the understanding that it is a gift and never to be repaid, and make sure the person understands this. ■

Mind Your Lifespan

Without a plan, we keep acting on our self-centered short-sightedness, forever working to pay bills that we accumulate as we buy more things that we think will help us enjoy life. Sadly, all we are really doing is sabotaging our life.

DO NOT LOSE perspective of your lifespan. We have a finite lifespan with various stages, and each is ideally suited for different purposes. For example, whenever we start to make gains to improve the quality of our lives and accumulate them, our remaining lifespan shortens and we reach a tipping point where further gains are not worth the cost. Consider this graph, in which strength and productivity are measured in terms of time and energy.

Assuming a lifespan of about one hundred years, our strength and productivity goes up sharply in our formative years then peaks and drops in a bell-like curve formation as we weaken and eventually die. The height of the curve represents our career success, and the area below represents our cumulative accomplishments. The earlier and sharper the rise, the larger the area under the curve becomes. Efforts made early in life will yield greater returns over the rest of your life. To achieve the same amount later in life may take a lot more effort (see line "b," 8 units, versus "a," 3 units of effort) at a time when it is harder to do and you would lose the gains in between as shown by the shaded area.

As you can see, it is best to work hard early on and accumulate the most until about your early forties, which is just at the

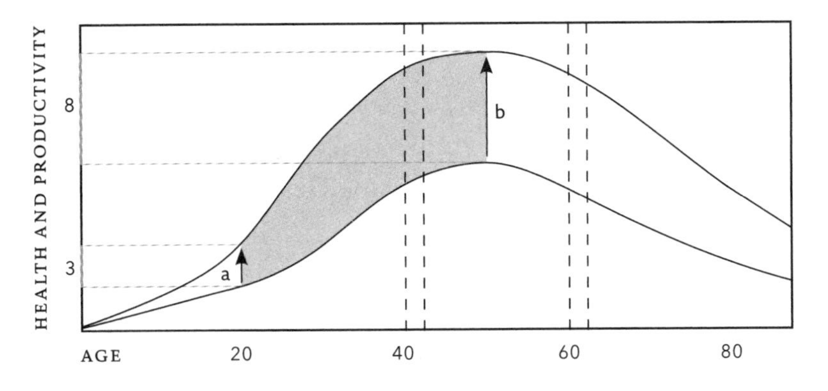

onset of your most productive years reaching a plateau. By this point, the returns from further career growth start to diminish because your remaining lifespan is shorter, and because our appreciation for more lessens as we accumulate more. At about this point it is wise to start focusing on enjoying life and being of service in a more spiritual way.

It will not matter whether you have a disposable income of $10,000 or $100,000 or $1 million per year, there is so much to enjoy that does not require money. We can develop our taste to fully enjoy life within any budget because the most important things in life are not material, such as nature, love for our family and friends, and helping society. The most important thing to develop at this point is a proper financial plan for a guaranteed lifelong income upon which you can build your life without worrying about your basic security. Without a plan, we keep acting upon our self-centered short-sightedness, forever working to pay bills for "more things" that we think will help us "enjoy life," while sadly all we are doing is sabotaging it. ■

What Is Success?

In some very important ways, life is similar to the game "Snakes and Ladders," as one turn or decision or even a thought process can pull you up or bring you down very far and very fast.

I HAVE OFTEN wondered if I would have been as successful if I had lived my life in accordance with the principles of this book instead of dedicating myself to working so hard in my early career. After all, I always attributed a great deal of my success to focus, dedication, and very hard work, sometimes working around the clock. So how could I have accomplished the same degree of success if I was fulfilled with the gifts of life that I already had?

The question most people would ask at this stage is: How does one define success? For example, is being rich and famous and powerful a real measure of success? Some would argue not, and others would argue that you are just trying to make yourself feel better about your lack of real success. I'd like to answer this question from a different angle and simply consider how life might have turned out differently for me had I always followed these principles.

For one, I would have slept well, eaten well, stayed active, and been as physically healthy as I could be. I would have also focused on my spirituality with meditation, spiritual meetings, and a personal support group. I would have had a much better perspective on life and lots of gratitude. I also believe that I would have been a lot sharper in my thinking, more balanced in my delivery, and a lot more effective in my ability to see and seize opportunities.

However, did my determination and brute hard work result in productivity that I could not otherwise achieve, or was this just another case of the tortoise versus the hare? Was it more effective to sprint for a while or to maintain a slower pace? The one thought that keeps coming to me is how in some very important ways life is similar to the game "Snakes and Ladders," as one turn or decision or even a thought process can pull you up or bring you down very far and very fast. For example, there is a much better chance that I would not have done drugs had I taken good care of myself. How much did I lose when the imbalance of my efforts caused my near-death collapse? Was I even a better man for it in the end?

I believe that if I had followed the principles of this book, putting my energy into taking better care of myself and enjoying life to the fullest while contributing more to my family and society, I would have made much better choices and become far more fulfilled with a lot less hardship. There is no question in my mind today that I would have been much more successful in every measure had I followed my principles as laid out in this book. ■

8 / Closing Thoughts

I learned that the meaning
of life is to live, to be invested
fully in the moment.

I FEEL BLESSED WITH THE COMFORT AND warmth of knowing that all I have to do is the next right thing and everything will be the best it can be and as it should be. Most people grasp how crucial it is for children to not miss out on their childhood, but we miss that it is equally crucial to not miss out on all of life, be it adolescence, middle age, old age, single life, married life, parenthood, or any other phase. Every stage is an incredible gift that must not be wasted or compromised in any way.

I learned that the meaning of life is not about fearing or dreaming or sacrificing to get somewhere better in the future, nor is it about dwelling and living in the memory of the past, no matter how beautiful or haunting it was. I learned what it is to live, to be invested fully in the moment. I know that I already have the best gifts and I trust that everything will turn out for the best, no matter what happens next.

When I finished my university studies, I often wondered what I had learned. There is no way that I could remember all of the minute details and formulas for everything from history to physics, math, or science. What I discovered is that I simply developed a second-nature understanding and intuitively knew the basics of how things work and where to look up the details as needed.

Today, I find that serenity has become second nature to me in a similar way. I discussed how I was able to find serenity after a major financial loss, but now I'm talking about a different level of serenity, one that is not tied to a particular event. It is serenity in every activity and at all times in my daily life without the fears and anxieties of thinking about what could have, should have, or would have been. It is a liberating surrender.

In the section "What Is Your Higher Purpose?" I discussed how animals are purely instinctual and far more spiritual than we could ever be. Ironically, I find that by living in the present I have come closer to their level of spirituality. Nonetheless, we have a superior intellect and it is healthy to have ambition for personal growth and a greater contribution to society, as long as it is not at the expense of the now. In other words, we can be extremely ambitious and invested in the process to achieve greatness without being invested in the outcome and getting lost in our anticipation.

Happiness and serenity have nothing to do with what happens to us and everything to do with the way we react to it. For example, if we have a negative experience, it might cause us to make a different important decision at some future point that could completely change our lives for the better, but if we react in anger, then out of spite and anger we might make a decision that is different from what life had intended for us.

Today, I am, for the most part, extremely happy and grateful. When I find myself struggling or without much enthusiasm despite all of my blessings, I remember that the vicissitudes are part of a natural cycle. I am also aware that I can lose my serenity and happiness if I do not take care of myself on a daily basis by structuring my priorities in my daily routine. First, I must nurture my health by staying active, eating healthy, resting well, and having regular checkups. Second, I must nurture my spirituality by pursuing my Higher Perspective, Power, and Purpose. Lastly, I must live my life to the fullest One Day at a Time.

There is no limit to how we can learn to fulfill our life on any given day. In fact, most of us spend many years in schools and colleges learning how to build a better life in the future, and I submit that it could take that much and more just to learn how to live a single day to the fullest. ■

Happiness

Happy people like the way things are and they look forward to change. Unhappy people don't like the way things are and they do not like change.

ONE DAY I bought delicious mangos that reminded me how much I enjoyed them when I was a child. I told my daughter to try one and she said, as she had many times before, that she does not like mangos. I convinced her they were different, and she tried one. She proceeded to enjoy the juices from the pit of the mango in the same way I remember doing as a child. She kept at it even when there was no fruit left, and I said, "This is just like I did as a child when the mangos were even better tasting." To which she replied, "How could they be better?" I laughed out of joy for her discovery of that beautiful flavor, but I also realized that this was how I feel now about my life.

I feel such joy and I attribute most of it to this faith that I am blessed with—knowing that everything will be great no matter what happens. In every aspect of my life, and in so many areas that I worried about before, I feel the serenity of just doing my best and what's right and knowing that everything will turn out great. That freed my mind to live in the moment. I feel so excited about my day. For example, I am about to meet my lawyer for a serious matter, yet I am looking forward to learning about what's new with him and his family. I am also going to my daughter's school where she will tell me about her day and I know I can be wholly present and capable of taking in so much and enjoying it all.

Living for the moment means having gratitude for the present time and faith that everything will be fine, no matter what happens. Even if bad things happen, they provide the opportunity for new ideas and improvement and growth. Take the example of having a house: wouldn't everyone like to have it changed and refreshed every so often? The same concept applies to everything in our lives. Growth comes from change, as does life.

Most unhappy people don't like the way things are for obvious reasons, but they also don't like change because they aren't ready for it. They do not live in the moment and are preoccupied by memories of the past and dreams or fears of the future. This does not allow them to pay attention to the present; change takes them by surprise and they don't deal well with it.

Conversely, happy people are serene with the way things are and have faith that no matter what happens, things will be good. This allows them to concentrate on the present and to make the best choices that leave them in the best shape to handle change properly. ■

As Good as It Gets

I was so full of gratitude for my awareness and knowledge that what I just experienced was magical, wonderful, and truly as good as it gets.

RECENTLY, I HAVE been enjoying wonderful evenings with my youngest daughter, Nyla. We talk and laugh all the time, and I feel involved in and aware of her life, her way of thinking, and her responses to things. One evening, she showed me a copy of a painting that she had submitted for a school project and told me that the school could use it to produce a personalized calendar but we would have to pay for it in the morning. She was so proud and explained how the copy did not do justice to the brilliant shades of yellow in her original painting, but which were sure to show up well on the final print. The next morning, we rushed to the front office to make the payment, but the administrative manager told us it was too late. My daughter became visibly shaken. I tried to console her, but she was turning deeper shades of red as she started to realize that her painting was lost forever.

She dug her face into my chest and cried quietly, at which point the school's principal passed by and asked what was wrong. I told her about my daughter's disappointment and that I was willing to drive the order over to the printing company. The principal asked us to follow her to the front office, where she asked the secretary to make the call to the printing company and to tell them that I was willing to deliver the form. After several tries she finally contacted them, and they agreed to accept the order later that day with the regular correspondence. They saved the day, and my daughter was relieved and happy.

As I left, I was overcome with feelings of gratitude for so many aspects of my time with my daughter. I was so grateful for how beautiful and healthy she is. So grateful for the fun that we had and the quality time that we spent together. So grateful for having been there to help her with something important to her and that she could not have done on her own. So grateful knowing that as she goes about her day and perhaps even forgets this whole incident, she will nonetheless always know in the back of her mind that her daddy was there when she needed him.

Many parents do that for their children, but what I am so full of gratitude for is my awareness that what I just experienced is magically wonderful and truly as good as it gets, and that my life had become so much more fulfilling. ■

Gratitude

Finding my Higher Perspective helped me to see life in a much wider context—with humility and knowledge that I am exactly where I am supposed to be. Finding my Higher Power helped me become connected and safe no matter what happens. Finding my Higher Purpose helped guide me to living life one day at a time with total fulfillment.

I WAS RECENTLY fortunate enough to attend a yoga retreat in the mountains of Julian, California. At night, our group gathered around a fire pit to share our experiences. As I sat there on the last night, listening to the crackling burning wood, I started to reflect on how far I had come from that little child whose fears of abandonment and impending doom dictated his emotions and reactions along the way.

How long had I traveled to reach this point in a far better place than where I started? I am no longer continuously ruled by my fears or my dreams. I am serene and content just being in the moment without worry or excitement about the past or the future. I am open to a deep love in my life like never before. I am the happiest I have ever been. There are always challenges, but with my Higher Perspective, Power, and Purpose, I know better than to try to change anything. I love life for what it is, no matter what it sends my way. I feel that is my greatest blessing.

At home, as I prepared to settle into my warm bed on a cold night, and as I thought about my beautiful family safe in their beds, I was fully aware of how blessed and wonderful this is.

Day after day, this beautiful existence has continued for some time, and although I realize it will not continue forever or even a long time, I am so blessed to have it now and I realize that I am in heaven. ■

Acknowledgements

/

TWO PEOPLE INSISTED I write a book about my life learnings. Thank you, Helen Scott Goudge, for your encouragement. And thank you, David Feder; you continue to help me grow my perspective and appreciate the gifts of life.

For shepherding me through the publishing labyrinth with the expertise and advice a first-time author needs, I thank Robert Mackwood of Seventh Avenue Literary Agency (and for introducing me to Robert, thanks to Jim Harris).

Alice Beck is a phenomenal editor, and her help with organizing the material is deeply appreciated. I'm also grateful for the way she connected with the book and believed in the message.

For their extremely customized approach and attention to the most minute of details, I thank Chris Labonté, Mark Redmayne, and Richard Nadeau of Figure 1 Publishing.

The beautiful design and style elements for this book were created by Jessica Sullivan. I thank her for her depth, vision, and inspiring creativity.

For her thoughtful copyediting, I'm thankful to Lesley Cameron.

With their creativity and design mojo, Jeniffer Thompson and her team at Monkey C have my deep thanks for building my website, www.higherbook.com.

Thanks also to Daniel Hunter, Sue Mitchell, and Mag Ruffman for the passion and vision that we share with *Higher*, and the creativity that they bring to the postproduction message and website design.

I'm thankful to some of my best friends who offered their feedback and constructive criticism as I worked through many drafts of my manuscript: thanks to all seventy of you! In particular, I'm grateful to Michael Khoury, Brad McAfee, Caroline Saad, Dalia Moftah, Dannah Everett, Dominique Russell, Fred Litwin, Grace Rigato, Heli Donaldson, Jim Hayward, Kristin Brin, Magda Hechema, Maggie Bras, Nancy Pencer, Ross Chevalier, Sheila Alofs, Stuart Hanna, Ted Warburton, Ted White, Therese Benimen, Valerie Ruescas, Vanessa Morcom, and Warren McCarthy.

To the treatment counselor who, in 1989, told me I had "tombstones for eyes," thank you for being the one who finally made me save my own life. And to the therapist who led me through my first Inner Child Meditation, it was life changing. Thank you.

To the members of my private support group, thank you for continually providing me with your insights and perspectives: Jim H., Ted W., Sean C., John M., and Douglas R. (may he rest in peace).

Thank you to my parents, who, in spite of their own deep wounds, provided me with their love and support. They were honest, kind people, and I grew up thinking everyone would be just like them, which actually resulted in some painful lessons! But all is well now, and I'm thankful for the example they set for me.

I also thank my sister Denise and my niece Hanna for their love and support.

I thank my daughter Nyla for always keeping me on my toes, and for her endless love for life, which keeps me grounded.

I also thank my son, Cameron, for his support and love.

And finally, I thank my aunt Jeanette and aunt Alice for always inspiring me, and for their endless love.

Index

/

"In today's world of nonstop distraction, this message can clearly serve as a helpful tool."—S. SPRALIJA

"It certainly made me stop and think, 'How does this apply to me and my life?' I hope Charles Hanna will continue what he is doing. Giving back is the beginning of becoming a whole human being."—M. DANIELS

"I sent the video link of this talk to all my friends. It is truly inspiring."—C. CHANG

"One of the best talks of this year's ideacity."—D. HUNTER

Continue the Journey
MORE THAN 40 MOVING AND CANDID VIDEO CLIPS
RICK BOSTON
WWW.HIGHERBOOK.COM
charles@HigherBook.com
• Find Higher resources on the web
• Read Charles' personal blog
• Explore media interviews and podcasts
• Learn about Charles' upcoming appearances, events, and his new book for young people
• Take the new Higher quiz to learn how your perceptual profile is influencing your life path

Charles Hanna's Talk at Ideacity

/

WHAT IS HAPPINESS? Is it what we get when we achieve our dreams? Isn't that why we work so hard to achieve them? Some people say that happiness is a state of mind. Others say that it is all about living in the moment. Harvard did an eighty-year study and concluded that happiness is about relationships and love. But if happiness is that simple, why is it so elusive? How come so many watch their lives race by while hoping that perhaps one day they will be truly happy? Even more perplexing is when we hear, "He did not know what he had until he lost it."

It seems that it's not just important to be happy but also to *know* when you are happy. Only then do we stop searching for more and start truly enjoying what we have. This is what happened to me, and I fell in love with my life. I am happier today than I have ever been, and I've been feeling this way for years. I believe that everyone can be, and deserves to be, really happy. Tonight I hope to offer valuable insight on how you can achieve greater happiness in your life regardless of your starting point.

Many of you will remember how in the early stages of space exploration everyone was fixated on reaching the moon. No one had any idea that the greatest discovery would be made not by viewing the moon close up, but by looking down at Earth from space.

Our planet was breathtaking. It put our world and life in a perspective no human had ever seen before. In a similar way, the treatment of addiction helped us gain a Higher Perspective on the origins of happiness. Studies show that addiction is a disease of perception, and recovery requires total mental surrender from a self-centered perspective to seeing oneself as part of something much bigger, like looking at Earth from space.

The rewards of surrender are priceless, but it is astonishingly scary and painful to do, as I personally experienced thirty years ago. I went into treatment for the sixth time after eight years of a deadly cocaine addiction. I weighed 127 pounds and was rabid with anger. It's a miracle I survived. For me it was a choice between total surrender and imminent death.

Why is surrender so hard? Imagine what it would be like to lose all your material and sentimental possessions. Now try to imagine another level altogether of having to give up all your intellectual and emotional possessions. Everything I ever knew was based on a reality that I had to abandon completely. Surrender is letting go of everything you believe in. How I saw myself, my parents, my soul mate, my daughter, and all my love and memories and ambitions and hopes—my sense of everything and everyone that I knew and lived for were gone!

But by totally surrendering, I began a journey into the unknown and found more beauty than I could have ever imagined. I discovered that almost everything we think we know about ourselves and our lives is a fabrication of our mind. That our mind is continuously distorting our reality to a point that is unrelated to our true existence. But just like in the movie *The Matrix*, when Neo woke up and found out he was living an alternate reality, we too have the capacity to wake up. Except in our case, our true existence is far more beautiful than what we have come to accept or even hope for.

Fortunately, you don't have to undergo this grueling surrender to benefit from those who have, just like you do not have to go to space to benefit from the discoveries made by those who did. So in the remaining twelve to thirteen minutes, I will share with you my discoveries and why they changed my life so much.

My first discovery was the value of my life.

I was always extremely ambitious and never satisfied. I believed it was a virtue to always strive for more, and that people would admire and embrace me for my accomplishments.

I started with a student loan and by the age of thirty I had built an iconic IT company and made millions. I had great friends, family, a beautiful daughter, and the absolute confidence that I would accomplish everything I set out to do and more. The result? I still felt unsatisfied—nothing changed. Everything felt the same. Success did not translate into that blissful happiness I expected. In fact, at the height of my success I felt lost for the first time, and my dissatisfaction fueled my abuse of drugs.

When you think about the tragic deaths of people even far more successful, you may ask, "How can they blow it after such success?" The answer, for me anyway, is that nothing is more valuable than the basic gifts of life that we are all born with. If something happens in our early development that robs us of our ability to enjoy those gifts, then no amount of wealth or fame or power or looks can make up for that loss.

What are these basic gifts of life? Well, how much would you sell your eyes for, or your abilities to hear, taste, touch, and smell? What about your health, freedom, and mobility; children, family, and friends? None of it would we sell—ever! Imagine having inconceivable riches in return for total isolation—never seeing, touching, or communicating with another human being for the rest of your life. Human contact alone is worth more than all the money there is. And there are so many other gifts!

Awakening to how priceless my life was, was my first clue that my mind was distorting my reality. I was fixated on pursuit of more, when nothing I could ever acquire could compare with what I had all along. And even when success did not bring me happiness, I still could not see it and felt lost!

My next discovery was my humanity.

About three months after I went into treatment, I was sitting in a large twelve-step meeting when I suddenly grasped that EVEN with my surrender, and even if I followed all the advice of my counselors, I might not make it. I was willing to do *anything* not to die, but I realized this might not be my choice anymore. And I just broke down and started to cry uncontrollably out of sorrow for myself, for my life, and for my little daughter.

I'll never forget that moment—people surrounded me and hugged me with unexpected love. I felt they truly wanted to save me, like they were saving themselves too. That made me think about how I had spent my whole life trying to be successful and attractive and funny so that people would like me. Well, here I was sobbing in this meeting, and I could not have been less attractive, ever. I was completely bankrupt in every sense, yet I had never felt such unconditional love, and from strangers.

My awakening was that I was loved simply because I am a human being. That's all. I did not need to be funny and attractive and successful to feel that love, to get that love. For the first time in my life, I saw what a gift it is just to be a human being, to be "one of us"!

You see, I was always too proud to ask for help. I did not feel entitled or want to appear needy. Suddenly, I realized I was entitled to be loved, like everyone else. I belonged. I could ask for help, and people would help me. My humility became my strength. I connected to our human experience, and that made me as strong as all humanity. That's when I knew I was going to be okay.

So, what is this Higher Perspective?

During the holidays I often found Christmas trees frustrating because they had flaws. The branches didn't spiral evenly and had big gaps and clumps that interfered with my perfect placement of ornaments.

But if we step back to look at a forest, the trees are perfect and countless creatures rely upon their natural formation to let the sun through and provide shelter. There is nothing that we could possibly do to make Mother Nature better.

Looking at one's life from a self-centered perspective is like seeing the flaws of a tree for something trivial like hanging ornaments. Every life, no matter how chaotic it looks close up, is a perfect piece of our much larger existence, like a tree in a forest. We are part of something much larger, which is breathtaking because it gave us life and everything we ever loved and cherished or can imagine in our wildest dreams.

Basically, we were each created in this life with specific attributes, in a specific place, at a specific time, and for what is obviously a specific purpose within the larger order. The more we are connected and in harmony with that, the more serene and fulfilled we become. Our Higher Perspective is our ability to see that our lives and everything that happens to us are part of this larger order. It helps us to live in serenity with the universe, instead of always trying to control everything to suit our self-centered perception.

Overly self-centered perception is a condition that I refer to as perception disorder. In the extreme, it manifests as addiction, depression, anxiety, and other mental health issues. But no one has perfect perception, and even a small distortion in our perception of reality compromises our ability to enjoy life to the fullest.

So how does perception disorder hurt us? It's a state of mind from which we evaluate everything by how it relates to us. If we are not invited to an event, we might conclude that the host does not like us. Or if our partner wants to talk to a friend in privacy, we might conclude that he or she must not trust us or wants to complain about us behind our back. When these imaginings are not true, they lead to distorted emotions and responses that break down our vital human connections.

Perception disorder begins during childhood if, for whatever reason, a child is not given adequate attention and time for regular intimate talks to help them understand the world and themselves and how to connect with others. If we, as children, do not receive this grounding, it forever distorts our perception and ability to truly connect with others, and over time, we become increasingly isolated and unhappy.

How do you know where you fit? If you want to know where you fall in the perception disorder spectrum, there is a free quiz on my website that asks questions like: Do you have resentments, keep secrets, or have difficulty trusting people? Have others described you as too sensitive, or say that you worry too much, or that you often seem angry? Do you take good care of your health? Regardless, if you find yourself often feeling unhappy or ungrateful, or even if you've just lost your joie de vivre, then you probably suffer from perception disorder to some degree.

Perception disorder is the root cause of the illusion that I referred to at the start. There are three parts to our illusion:

The first part is the illusion that we own our lives.

Did you ever wonder why we paid nothing for our lives, when it takes years just to pay for a car or house? We have no say when, or how long, or if we live at all. This life is not ours—it's entrusted to us for a short period of time. But our minds give us the *illusion* that we own our lives. We feel shame or pride, and seek recognition for something we never created or deserve credit for. As a result, instead of feeling inherently happy and connected like a tree in a forest, sadly, we become anxious and increasingly isolated by constantly comparing ourselves to others.

The second part of our illusion is that we take our life gifts for granted.

Our minds tune out all constants—like a hum that we become aware of only when it stops. That is why we have to lose a gift to appreciate its importance. So instead of completely embracing what gifts we have now, we are easily distracted by petty activities and thoughts of future plans, and we squander the most precious moments of our lives.

The third part of our illusion is that we would be happy if only things were different.

Our world can change any day for any reason. Even what we fight for can easily turn out to be bad for us and vice versa. Yet our mind keeps telling us that we *can* and *must* control our world to be happy. Meanwhile, each new day brings life's intended challenges and opportunities, and instead of embracing them, we are alienated because we are preoccupied with our own plans. As a result, we make big mistakes and miss the best opportunities.

And it's easy to buy these illusions because society also baits our egos with glamorized images and messages, forever luring us into believing that to be truly happy we must be richer, skinnier, sexier, younger, faster, powerful, famous, gifted, and always deserving of instant relief and gratification.

At the beginning I made you a promise—that we have the capacity to wake up, and the rewards are mind blowing. I wrote *Higher* to show how we can align our lives in simple but crucial ways to offset the negative effects of perception disorder and live a more fulfilling life.

Imagine being completely at peace with yourself and living in the moment so that time seems to stand still. Your brain is quiet and able to savor every minute detail of your priceless gifts. Imagine every new day borne on a fresh blank canvas, with life ready to paint a new masterpiece not blemished with your fears, or even dreams, like ornaments on a tree. Every day, real, fresh, exciting, engaging, with new opportunities for you to grow, fall in love, whatever you desire.

Higher shows how being connected to something much bigger brings clarity regardless of your belief system. You will see yourself as a trusted guardian of your life with gratitude that erases all fear and anger. Your deeper connection with people will give you insight and help you eliminate the resentments and secrets that isolate us, and you will enjoy each day fully knowing that tomorrow will be even better.

I leave you with this parting thought:

When you let go of self-centeredness, you connect with something much larger. And it feels like coming home.

Thank you.

WATCH THE VIDEO ONLINE AT
CHARLESHANNA.COM/IDEACITY.

About the Author

/

CHARLES HANNA is the Chairman, CEO, and founder of a third-party technology provider that he began in a basement in 1979 and built into a leading service consolidation company with offices across Canada. A devoted father of three children, Hanna is involved with a range of charities, including organizations that help with cancer treatment, Canadian artists, and displaced and handicapped people. He has a particular soft spot for children and animals, and contributes his personal time in various ways to the YMCA and animal shelter groups. He divides his time between Toronto and LA.